40 *Days* to Embrace
Your Encounter with the Lord

Not Defined
by the *Struggle*

DeAnna D. Cavenah

Copyright © 2022 DeAnna Cavenah

Amplified Bible Scripture quotations marked "AMP" are taken from the Amplified® Bible, Copyright © 1954, 1958, 1962, 1964, 1965, 1987 by The Lockman Foundation. Used by permission. New International Version Scripture quotations marked (NIV) are taken from the Holy Bible, New International Version®, NIV®. Copyright © 1973, 1978, 1984 by Biblica, Inc.™ Used by permission of Zondervan. All rights reserved worldwide. New Living Translation Scripture quotations marked (NLT) are taken from the Holy Bible, New Living Translation, copyright © 1996, 2004, 2007 by Tyndale House Foundation. Used by permission of Tyndale House Publishers, Inc., Carol Stream, Illinois 60188. All rights reserved. The Message Scripture quotations marked "MSG" or "The Message" are taken from The Message. Copyright 1993, 1994, 1995, 1996, 2000, 2001, 2002. Used by permission of NavPress Publishing Group. The Passion Translation Scripture quotations marked "TPT" are from The Passion Translation®. Copyright © 2017, 2018 by Passion & Fire Ministries, Inc. Used by permission. All rights reserved. No part of this document may be reproduced or transmitted in any form or by any means, electronic, mechanical, photocopying, recording, or otherwise, without prior written permission of the author.

NOT DEFINED BY THE STRUGGLE
40 Days to Embrace Your Encounter with the Lord

DeAnna Cavenah
Passionate4Praise@yahoo.com

ISBN 978-1-949826-43-2
Printed in the USA.
All rights reserved

Author photograph by:
Hadley Paige Photography: Hadleypaige17161.Wixsite.com

Published by: EAGLES GLOBAL BOOKS | Frisco, Texas
In conjunction with the 2022 Eagles Authors Course
Cover & interior designed by DestinedToPublish.com

Dedication

First and foremost I dedicate this book to Jesus, my Lord and Savior. None of this is possible without you. My desire is to reveal your heart and represent you well as your beloved daughter.

Secondly, to all of my readers. My prayer is that you hear my heart in each devotion encouraging you to keep moving forward, no matter what season of life you find yourself in. Jesus, who is the author and finisher of your faith, will complete the work that He has begun in you.

> *"I am convinced and confident of this very thing, that He who has begun a good work in you will [continue to] perfect and complete it until the day of Christ Jesus [the time of His return]."*
> —Philippians 1:6 (AMP)

Acknowledgments

To my husband, Greg: You have always been my greatest supporter. Your words to me on the day I approached you about writing this devotion will always ring loud in my ears. You said without hesitation, "Go for it!" I can't thank you enough for your confidence in me. I couldn't have accomplished this without you by my side.

To my son Ethan: For all of those days you wondered if I would ever come out of the room, thank you! For the mornings that you settled for a honey bun for breakfast because Momma had a deadline to meet, thank you! For giving me another 15 minutes, 30 minutes, or hour, thank you! Thank you for all of your patience and understanding.

To my son Michael: Ever since you were a little boy, you always saw your momma chase after her dreams, so when I told you I was writing a book, you never questioned or doubted me. Thank you for always being a sounding board and for all of your ideas for the book title.

To my mom and dad: Thank you for raising me to be a God-fearing woman. Thank you for always standing by my side and believing in me.

I love you!

Acknowledgments

To all of my friends and church family who have prayed for me, loved me, and encouraged me through this process of becoming a first-time published author, thank you!

To that certain friend, you know who you are, that told me, "You don't have to write the whole book at once. Just start with the first page."

You gave me the courage to start.

To my niece Hadley: As your Nanny, I'm forever grateful to you for believing in me. Thank you for allowing the Lord to use you to be His voice to me when I needed a direction. Thank you for the amazing photo shoot.

To my very special friend, Cherie Forsythe: It's been quite a journey that we have traveled together these past couple of years. We have ventured out into some uncharted territory, and we have victoriously made it to the other side. You've been a listening ear, a shoulder to lean on, and most importantly an amazing prayer partner.

Looking forward to our next adventure together.

To my instructor, Marilyn Alexander: I am forever grateful that our paths crossed. I felt a connection the first time I spoke to you at Summit. Thank you for all that you do for every one of your authors. Thank you for believing in us and giving us the confidence to "just keep writing."

To my writing coaches, Deborah Anthony and Kara May: Thank you for being my midwives. The labor was hard, but you helped me push this baby out. Thank you for asking the hard questions, for helping me understand the why behind my why, and for encouraging me to find my voice. I am forever grateful for all of the hours you poured into me. You both are a well of knowledge and jewels in the Kingdom.

Preface

If there is one thing I know for certain, it's that now is the time for you and me to live life with passion on purpose.

How do we live a life with passion on purpose? By making a choice to be intentional and continue to stir up the gifts within us. We must choose to embrace and encounter Jesus no matter what season of life we find ourselves in.

I've been journaling for years, but I never saw myself as a writer, let alone an author. In the past few years, however, I've felt a strong desire to put those journal entries into a devotion. I began to realize that now was the time to give birth to all of those things that I had been carrying in my spiritual womb. I knew that it would help stir up hope, joy, passion, and encouragement within others. Over the next 40 days, you will take a journey into the seasons of my heart. A journey of early morning devotion times as I seek the heart, mind, and will of God for my life. Late nights of being awakened by Holy Spirit in order for Him to spend time with me, giving me new perspective and fresh vision for the days ahead. I pray you will be blessed in this journey.

Table of Contents

Introduction 1
Day 1: The Dress 3
Day 2: Just This One Time 7
Day 3: Filtering Pain through Prayer 10
Day 4: The Gift of Laughter 13
Day 5: Remove Dead Things 17
Day 6: Let Go! 20
Day 7: Choose Joy! 24
Day 8: The Dash in the Middle 26
Day 9: Stronger Than the Struggle 30
Day 10: Embrace Change 33
Day 11: Dirt Under the Rug 36
Day 12: The Crucible 39
Day 13: Transformation! 43
Day 14: The R.A.W. Truth: Real, Authentic, and Worthy ... 46
Day 15: Flip the Script! 51
Day 16: Don't Back Down! 54

Day 17: Hold the Rope...........................57
Day 18: Relinquish Control......................60
Day 19: Pause and Be Still......................63
Day 20: R.I.P.—Rest in Peace...................67
Day 21: Seasons................................71
Day 22: The Greatest Commandment...............75
Day 23: God Is Close to the Broken-hearted.....79
Day 24: Don't Disqualify Yourself!.............83
Day 25: Entangled..............................87
Day 26: Basking in His Presence................91
Day 27: Begin with Thankfulness................94
Day 28: Yield My Heart.........................98
Day 29: Distractions! Distractions!...........101
Day 30: Don't Despise Where You Are...........105
Day 31: It's Time to Possess!.................108
Day 32: From Pain to Purpose..................111
Day 33: Take Off the Limits...................114
Day 34: Not Forgotten!........................118
Day 35: Find Your Anchor......................121
Day 36: The Power of Choice...................125
Day 37: Guard and Harden Not Your Heart.......129
Day 38: There Is More.........................132
Day 39: Present in the Moment.................135
Day 40: Victory in Every Season...............138

Introduction

Have you ever noticed that just as earth has four seasons, winter, spring, summer, and fall, our personal lives go through seasons and cycles as well? Unlike earth's seasons that last for a specified time, the seasons of our life are much more unpredictable. Your winter season could be cold, dry, and lonely, seeming to last months or even years. On the contrary, it could be that you have a very short winter, and spring came more quickly with vibrancy and much growth. Whatever season of life you find yourself in today, one thing I continue to learn is that every season has an ending, and after every storm, the sun shines again. There is beauty to be found and lessons to be learned as you lean in and embrace each season of your life.

> *"It's a new season. A perfect opportunity to do something new, something bold, something beautiful!"*
> —Anonymous

Through this journey called life, I have experienced many seasons of uncertainty, brokenness, and disappointment. However, in the midst of it all, I've also experienced much joy, peace, and restoration. God has shown me that nothing we ever go through is wasted. He has given me beauty for ashes, joy for mourning, and

Introduction

purpose and praise for pain. I'm going to share some inspirational stories and many testimonies of the faithfulness of God as He has brought me through each of those seasons. I want you to realize, my friend, that you are stronger than the struggle. You are not holding this devotion by accident. As you set your face like flint, determined to do His will, and live a life with intentionality, He will take you on a journey full of passion and purpose. As you embrace each encounter with the Lord, He will take you deeper into His heart, revealing so much more than what is actually happening to you on the surface.

So, as we journey together through this daily devotion, it is my prayer that your faith grows bigger than any trial you experience. God wants you to live on mission, fulfilling all that He has called you to do.

So, go ahead, grab your Bible and a pen, and find a quiet place to begin our journey. I've pulled together some of my favorite quotes, scriptures, confessions, and life lessons. I've also provided thought-provoking questions, space for your personal reflection, and scriptures to take you on a deeper journey into God's Word. In the "Worship Encounter" section at the end of each chapter, you'll find my suggestions for worship songs that will give you time for His presence to take you into an encounter that will shift your atmosphere.

Remember that He causes everything to work together for your good (Romans 8:28).

I believe in you!

DeAnna

DAY 1

THE DRESS

"God blesses us more so that we can be more of a blessing to others."

—**Mark Batterson**

One time, a few years ago, I bought a dress without trying it on at the store. When I got home, you guessed it, it didn't fit. I felt if I could just lose a little bit of weight, then it would fit. But it was odd—no matter how much weight I lost, it still would not fit. I decided that I would obviously never wear it. Sometimes I take my clothes to a couple little resale shops to earn a little extra spending cash. I just knew that one of the stores would want the dress because it still had the tags on it and it was super cute. But to my surprise, neither store wanted to purchase it. So I brought it back home and put it back in my closet, thinking again, "I'll just lose a few more pounds, and possibly it will fit." By faith, I even purchased some shoes to match the dress. Every dress needs the perfect shoes.

Several days later, while getting ready for church, I decided to take the dress off the hanger. I just knew it would fit—and besides, I now had the perfect shoes. When I put the dress on, I looked in the mirror and said, "This isn't even my dress! This belongs to Martha" (name changed to respect my friend). I put it in a bag and was determined that she would leave church with it. After church as I was handing her the bag, I held on to it while explaining the story about the dress. Surprisingly, she said, "Okay, I need to tell you something, and I'm about to cry." She proceeded to tell me about a dream she had that she had gone into my closet and was trying on my clothes. In the dream, my little boy and I came home, and she got very nervous and felt very ashamed of herself. She began to take the clothes off and hurried up to put her own clothes back on. There were a few more details about her dream that she shared, along with her own interpretation of it, but I will leave that out for the sake of reading and also to respect her privacy.

I looked at her and said, "Well, there's no more shame, this is rightfully yours." On the drive home, I started really thinking about the dream that she shared with me and how, in a split second, the Holy Spirit had whispered to me, "This isn't your dress."

I feel this story has a couple of different meanings.

#1- The dress I purchased was never meant to be mine. I'm convinced I would never have lost enough weight for it to fit, and it would never have sold.

Sometimes God wants to use us like a conduit—a means of transmitting or distributing. Could it be that God wants to use you to help strengthen another person's faith, bless them, or confirm something to them? It's twofold, for you and the other person. If it brings stress to your life or is uncomfortable, take some time to consider if it's really yours.

#2- Referring to my friend's dream, I think sometimes as Christians, we go into our prayer closet (wherever that might be) and the Lord begins to reveal to us all that He has for us, but it's hard for us to receive because of shame, guilt, and feelings of unworthiness. So we try it on, but then quickly take it off and put our old clothes back on. The truth is, you are worthy of everything He has to give you, not because of anything you did but because of what He did for you on the cross. He took on your guilt and shame so you wouldn't have to carry it, and He made you righteous—in right standing with Him. Let Him dress you today!

> *"I am overwhelmed with joy in the Lord my God! For he has dressed me with the clothing of salvation and draped me in a robe of righteousness. I am like a bridegroom dressed for his wedding or a bride with her jewels."*
> —Isaiah 61:10 (NLT)

Pause and Reflect:

1. What are you trying to hold on to and make fit in your life?

   _____

   _____

2. What is it that God has said is yours but you feel unworthy to receive?

   _____

   _____

Go Deeper:

Acts 20:35 (NLT)

Worship Encounter:

"I Give Myself Away" by William McDowell

"Clean" by Natalie Grant

"Priceless" by For King & Country

"Grave Clothes" by Tribl Records (feat. Jessica Hitte & Montel Moore)

DAY 2

JUST THIS ONE TIME

"Little foxes spoil the vines. And little sins do much harm to the tender heart."

—Charles Spurgeon

I've been trying to lose the unnecessary 10 pounds that seems to continually hang around. As I was thinking about the day ahead of me, one of the things on my to-do list was to go to a friend's housewarming. My mind immediately shifted to all of the food that would be there, which, by the way, is my favorite kind of food. I always justify myself by saying, "This is a special event, it won't hurt this one time, I'll start over tomorrow." But as I sat there, something different came out of my mouth that sounded like this: "I don't have to eat everything that is set in front of me." Now, if I were on a mission trip, that would be different, but that's another story for another time. I wish I had the testimony that I passed the test, but I did eat a cupcake.

I started thinking about how, as Christians, we often just partake of anything and everything that is set before us. "That movie that only has a few curse words and a couple of nude scenes, surely this one time won't hurt me." What about that song that has an awesome beat that gets you dancing, but the lyrics are so provocative that you would never dare speak them out loud? I know that those are extreme examples, but what about something a little less obvious like receiving too much change back at the cash register, or spending time with friends and beginning to gossip about another friend? Oh, that's right, "we weren't really gossiping, we were just concerned and we needed to pray for her." What about this one: not keeping your first commitment because something else better came along? Ouch, that one hurt. Well, the list could go on and on. Regardless of what it is, that adopted mindset of "it won't hurt this one time" could turn into a very unhealthy lifestyle affecting every area of your life and most importantly your spirit. Today, together, let's make a decision to keep our physical and spiritual life healthy.

Pause and Reflect:

1. Ask yourself if you have allowed little things to come into your life that could rob what God has planted within you.

   _____

   _____

2. How would this affect you spiritually?

   _____

   _____

3. Identify a time in your life when you said, "Just this one time won't hurt."

   _____

   _____

Go Deeper:

Song of Songs 2:15 (TPT), 1 Timothy 4:8 (NLT), 1 Corinthians 10:31 (TPT), Matthew 6:22 (AMP)

Worship Encounter:

"Heaven Help Me" by Zach Williams

"Thank God for Sunday Morning" by Cochren & Co.

"Fresh Start" by Ryan Stevenson

DAY 3

FILTERING PAIN THROUGH PRAYER

"No man can do me a truer kindness in this world than to pray for me."

—**Charles Spurgeon**

Have you ever had days when you are feeling oppressed, depressed, or a little discouraged for no apparent reason? You can't understand what is going on, and you tell yourself, "I shouldn't be feeling this way."

Think about this: it may be that you are carrying someone else's burden. Stop for a moment, and instead of sinking into a world of self-defeat and despair, sink to your knees in prayer. Although you are possibly carrying another person's burden, this in itself is not a burden, but a precious gift called intercession. God has entrusted you, my dear friend, at that moment to filter that pain, their pain, through prayer. Intercession by definition is the action of saying a prayer on behalf of another, or as some would say, "standing in the gap" for them. A dear minister friend of ours mentioned in a recent service, "God will begin to give you keys to unlock doors for other people."

Well, yesterday was one of those days that I had been given a key. The sad thing about it was, I didn't realize I held that key until 12:45 in the morning, when the Holy Spirit gently woke me up from a deep sleep to begin to speak to me about the words I am penning now. He began with "Learn to filter your pain through prayer." After that, my day began to unfold before me, and at that moment, I had that "Aha, now I understand" feeling. I knew exactly who I was carrying, but I hadn't discerned the key that was placed in my hand, and therefore, I missed a precious opportunity to unlock the door for that person through prayer. My God is such a merciful and loving Father to wake me up to reveal this specific truth to me—a truth that I've known and even shared with others, but yet I missed it. Let it be an "aha" moment for you as well as you learn to filter that unexplained emotional pain through prayer. The Lord is handing out keys in this season. Will you discern how to use that key?

PAUSE AND REFLECT:

1. Have you had some unexplained or unsettling feelings of depression or discouragement lately? If so, how would you describe it?

_____

_____

2. Do you feel this is for you personally, or are you possibly carrying someone else's burden?

   _____

   _____

3. Whether or not the Holy Spirit has shown you that this is for you or for a specific person, go ahead right now and use your key to unlock some doors through prayer.

   _____

   _____

Go Deeper:

Galatians 6:2 (AMP), 1 John 5:14 (TPT), Job 42:10 (NLT)

Worship Encounter:

"Standing in the Gap" by Babbie Mason

"In Jesus Name" by Katy Nichole

"Somebody's Praying Me Through" by Allen Asbury

DAY 4

The Gift of Laughter

"There is nothing in the world so irresistibly contagious as laughter and good humor."
—**Charles Dickens**

Sometimes we have to give people what they don't even realize they need.

The Bible says, *"A happy heart is good medicine and a joyful mind causes healing, but a broken spirit dries up the bones"* (Proverbs 17:22 AMP).

In The Passion Translation, the same verse reads like this: *"A joyful, cheerful heart brings healing to both body and soul. But the one whose heart is crushed struggles with sickness and depression."*

As I pondered upon a recent family gathering that I would be hosting, I felt the need to bring laughter into the room. As Holy

Spirit began speaking to me about this, I remembered a couple of games that I had played before at other parties. Not only would they bring laughter but they would bring unity as well. I wasn't sure how I would be received when I presented the games; after all, we had never done this before that I could remember. Was I setting myself up to be rejected? What if no one was interested in playing games? What if they were beyond broken and didn't care to participate in anything?

I had to press through all of the "what ifs," fears, and doubts.

One of the many things I've learned on my journey with the Holy Spirit is that if He is speaking it to you and can get it through you, then He will breathe on it.

As I scanned the room, I was reminded of just how much everyone had gone through just within the last 12 months.

There had been death and much grief associated with death. A horrible car accident that led to multiple surgeries. Another car accident that left minor injuries but much trauma. Separations and divorces, injuries, sickness, depression, anxiety, ADHD, battles in the mind, fears of job loss, and the list could go on. Let's face it, there are some serious issues that will crush anyone's spirit. I knew the best gift that I could offer in the moment was the gift of laughter.

Now it was time to take the leap of faith. As it came out of my mouth, "Let's play a game," without hesitation they asked, "What kind of game?" and to my surprise, everyone was on board. As everyone gathered together and began to laugh and have fun, it's like I could see heavy burdens begin to lift in that very moment. As I offered this gift of joy, I too felt refreshed in my spirit.

After the games had stopped, the laughter continued on. It's important to know and have confidence in what you carry and to be obedient to the voice of the Holy Spirit. One act of obedience can shift the entire atmosphere.

> "One act of obedience can shift the entire atmosphere."

PAUSE AND REFLECT:

1. What is it that you carry on the inside that could help bring laughter to someone broken and crushed in spirit by the weight of life's struggles?

   _____

   _____

2. How could your simple act of obedience shift the atmosphere of a situation or a certain person's life?

   _____

   _____

GO DEEPER:

Isaiah 61:1-3 (NLT), Job 8:21 (NLT), Psalm 30:11 (AMP), Psalm 42:5 (AMP)

Worship Encounter:

"Laughter" by BeBe Winans

"Confident" by Steffany Gretzinger

"Never Run Dry" by Matt Gilman

DAY 5

REMOVE DEAD THINGS

> What you allow in your life determines what grows within you!

Recently as I walked past one of my plants, I noticed it had a few dead leaves on it. As I pulled them out, the Lord began to speak to me about dead things—how they serve no purpose and have no place in our lives.

Just like we must get the dead leaves off of our plants in order for them to grow, it's time to pull out the dead things in our life that are no longer serving a purpose and are not beneficial to our growth. If a plant has dead leaves, you will automatically be drawn to that dead leaf. It has changed colors, and it just hangs there. It's not going to produce or add to the beauty of that plant. What once was beautiful has become unattractive. If not pulled out or cut away, it will eventually spread to the rest of the plant, causing infection and stunting its growth, and soon it will begin to wither away. So it goes with our life: if we allow these dead, non-producing things to remain in our lives, we will soon become unproductive and unattractive to those who look upon us.

Are there areas in your life today that need to be tended to? Maybe you need to get rid of some things that have been hanging around that have no life or beauty in them. Maybe it's some habits. It could be things that clutter your life. Maybe it's some relationships that need to be cut away from your life. Not to sound mean, but there are some relationships that will suck the life out of you and leave you feeling dry and withered. Maybe you need to set some healthy boundaries. What do people see when they look at you? Beauty, or dead things?

Another thought is the watering process. When I brought my plant in, it looked as if it was wilting. I felt the soil, and it was dry. I had not watered it in a while. Before I went to bed, I watered it well, and when I got up the next morning, all of its leaves were stretched high as if giving praise to God. So it goes with our life: if we do not stay in the word of God and let it wash over us and get into the soil of our spirit, then we will become dry and joyless. We will wake up one day and feel so down that we have a hard time looking up.

It's time to check your soil. Have you neglected it? Have you watered it with the Word and bathed it in His Presence? Take care of your spiritual walk with the Lord. You are the only one responsible for your life, how you live, how you grow, and how you represent yourself before those around you. People need to see the beauty of Jesus in you.

Pause and Reflect:

1. Can you identify some dead things that are no longer serving a purpose in your life?

   _____

   _____

2. Are there areas of your life where you need to set up healthy boundaries?

   _____

   _____

Go Deeper:

2 Corinthians 3:18 (NLT), Ephesians 2:10 (NLT), Colossians 3:16-17 (TPT)

Worship Encounter:

"Springtime" by Chris Renzema

"Isaiah Song" by Maverick City Music (feat. Chandler Moore)

"Do They See Jesus in Me?" by Joy Williams

"Your Nature" by Kari Jobe

DAY 6

LET GO!

"Anything you can't control in life is teaching you how to let go."

—Unknown

Have you ever had someone tell you, "Just let go"? It's easy for them to say, because they aren't the ones in the situation. More often than not, letting go is hard, but it can be done. It's another one of those choices we make. Letting go is an obedient act of faith.

I've had to choose to let go of many things in my life that I could not control. This, in my opinion, is one of the very things that tries to steal your joy: trying to control situations and circumstances, not only in your life but in the lives of other people as well. There are some things that you simply cannot change. God is ultimately the one who is in control of every aspect of our lives. What we do oftentimes is take that control out of His hands and try to play God. That never works! When we do this, it basically delays the process, and we prolong the outcome. It's important that we yield to the process. I believe that as we release control, we allow joy to function in our lives.

The joy of the Lord is our strength, according to Nehemiah 8:10. I don't know about you, but I don't want to spend one more day on the hamster wheel, running in circles, wearing myself out, and never getting anywhere. We think we know what's best for our lives and the lives of our loved ones, but God has every single day numbered, and He knows the ultimate plan.

In Nehemiah, the people wept when they heard God's laws and realized how far they were from obeying them. Isn't that just like us? We hear God's word and know what to do, but our lack of trust turns into disobedience, therefore causing us to be sad and weak.

Instead, let's choose to cast all of our cares, worries, and daily struggles upon Christ, just like His Word tells us. We are strengthened spiritually and filled with joy when we choose this way of living.

My friend, today let's look to the Author and Finisher of our faith, trust Him, and let go!

Pause and Reflect:

1. Have you allowed a situation in your life to zap your strength?

_____

_____

2. How would this situation look if you chose to let go and release control?

   _____

   _____

3. Make this declaration today:
   I choose to put it back in the hands of the Lord and trust that He is working it all out for the good of those involved.

Go Deeper:

Hebrews 12:2 (AMP), 1 Peter 5:7 (AMP), Romans 8:28 (AMP)

Worship Encounter:

"Spirit Lead Me" by Michael Ketterer & Influence Music

"Letting Go" by Steffany Gretzinger

"I'm Gonna Let It Go" by Jason Gray

"Let Go, Let God" by Jack Cassidy

Let Go!

DAY 7

CHOOSE JOY!

"Joy is not in things, it is in us."
—Richard Wagner

Every morning when I wake up, one of the first things I do is open all of the blinds in my home. I've made this a daily practice in my life. It's amazing how this simple act lifts me up! I CHOOSE to dwell in the light, and not in darkness! I CHOOSE JOY even on days when I don't feel it!

It's important that we don't confuse joy with happiness. Happiness is connected to what is going on around us, and it gets mixed up in our emotions. Joy, however, is connected to our relationship with the Lord and is not affected by our difficult circumstances. You can have joy in spite of the storms you may be facing. Joy is one of the nine fruits of the Spirit. It's already inside of us; we just need to make a decision to surrender to it. Choose joy today and every day! Joy is an act of obedience. Do something today that you have never done before! Open your blinds! Reach out to someone today through text, email, phone call, a card, or a visit and watch your joy level increase!

Pause and Reflect:

1. Can you see where you may have confused joy with happiness?

   _____

   _____

2. Can you identify some things you can do differently that will cause you to connect with the joy of the Lord?

   _____

   _____

3. Can you think of someone you can reach out to today who needs joy?

   _____

   _____

Go Deeper:

Galatians 5:22-23 (AMP), Nehemiah 8:10 (AMP), Psalm 30:5 (AMP)

Worship Encounter:

"Joy" by For King & Country

"Joy" by Jonny Diaz

"Joy" by Highlands Worship

DAY 8

THE DASH IN THE MIDDLE

"There'll be two dates on your tombstone and all your friends will read 'em, but all that's gonna matter is that little dash between 'em."

—**Kevin Welch**

I'm sure you've had those nights when you just didn't sleep well—tossing and turning with thoughts running through your mind. That was me last night. As I sit here writing this daily devotion, drinking my coffee, tears are welling up in my eyes, and I feel such heaviness.

Can we talk for a few moments about what's going on? Let's talk about death. I know, it's not a real popular subject, but it is inevitable, and I don't think it's discussed enough. We talk and post on social media about "living our best life" or "living life to the fullest," etc., but what about "life after death"?

We go about our day, and then days turn into weeks, weeks turn into months, and months turn into years of trying to live our best life and get ahead. We set goals and try to achieve them: paying off debt, driving a nice car, building our dream home, making sure our families are doing well, and the list goes on.

Please don't misunderstand me here! I have done and still do these things, and there is nothing wrong with them—they are great goals, and a part of all of our lives.

Let's think together about what I'm saying for a moment. You see, the same God that gave you life knows your end from your beginning. All of our days are numbered here on earth. We all have an appointment with death. Death is final here on earth, and it's a very sad day for those left behind who grieve the death of a loved one. But death is not final for the child of God. We have been promised Eternal Life! We will all have two dates on our tombstone: the day we were born, and then our final resting date. What matters most is the dash in the middle. How did we live the dash? What decisions were made with the dash?

So, why couldn't I sleep last night? Why such heaviness this morning?

You see, a week ago, I lost my niece to death, and tomorrow we say our final goodbyes here on earth. She was very young, and it seemed like she had her whole life ahead of her. I do have the assurance that she called upon the name of the Lord and she no longer has pain or struggles. Even so, death is never easy.

You see, one of the greatest weapons of the enemy is to suggest to you that you have plenty of time to get your life right. He will tell you, "Live life however you want to live it—it's your life." My niece had just turned 21, and the truth is, you don't know your death date. When your mother was pregnant with you, the doctors gave her a due date or a roundabout day of your birth, but none of us know the day we will die. Never assume you are okay with God. Being good and doing good works doesn't get you to Heaven. It's accepting Jesus as your personal Savior and living your life for Him. If you even question your salvation today, then it's a good day to make sure. You'll have a new birthday. You'll be "born again" of the Spirit. It's your spirit that lives for eternity, not this earthly flesh. One day, you will exchange your earthly flesh suit for a crown in Heaven. I always tell my boys, "Live today as if it were your last."

Be sure and pray this prayer:

Father, I acknowledge today that I am in need of a Savior. I believe Jesus Christ is your Son. I believe that He died on a cross for my sins and that you raised Him back to life. I ask for forgiveness today and ask Jesus to come live in my heart to be my Lord and Savior from this day forward. I am now a child of God. Amen.

Pause and Reflect:

1. Considering the dash in the middle, how will you choose to live it out?

   _____

   _____

2. Have you confused getting to Heaven with good works, or do you truly have a relationship with the Lord?

_____

_____

Go Deeper:

2 Corinthians 5:17 (AMP), James 4:14 (AMP), 2 Corinthians 6:1-2 (AMP), John 3:3 (AMP)

Worship Encounter:

"Getting Ready" by Maverick City Music feat. UPPERROOM

"Build My Life" by Pat Barrett

"Give My Life To You/Our King Has Come" by Elevation Worship

DAY 9

STRONGER THAN THE STRUGGLE

"The next time you're disappointed, don't panic and don't give up. Just be patient and let God remind you He's still in control."

—Max Lucado

> "God will not allow you to go through anything without it having a purpose."

Let's be honest! There are some days it would just be easier to say, "I give up!" "I quit!" "I'm done!" Those days when you've given your all, but it doesn't feel like it was enough. The days that feel like you have been kicked in the gut. The days when everyone else seems to be happy and moving forward while you seem to be going in reverse. The struggle is real, yes, but friend, let me tell you that God is so much more REAL! And you are much stronger than the struggle! God will not allow you to go through anything without it having a purpose. He wastes nothing! Yes, even those things that make absolutely no sense. He is using even these things to work in your favor.

There is greatness in you! There is gold in you! Let Him dig it out, no matter the cost! The enemy gets too much praise and glory. Not everything that happens to you is of the enemy. Remember, it's not what happens *to* you but what happens *in* you. Pause! It's possible that God has allowed some chaos in your life so that you will become totally dependent on Him, because if it wasn't for Him, you would not come through. Trust Him in the middle of it all.

Pause and Reflect:

1. Can you identify how the Lord might be purging some things in you so that the pure gold can come forth in you?

　
　

2. Will you still be found faithful in the middle of the struggle surrounding your life?

3. Could it be that this isn't even about you but about the people He is sending you to? Who needs to hear your story?

_____

_____

Go Deeper:

James 1:2-4 (TPT), Romans 8:28 (AMP), Psalm 34:18-19 (NLT)

Worship Encounter:

"Stronger" by Mandisa

"Stronger" by Influence Music & Matt Gilman

"You're Gonna Be OK" by Brian & Jenn Johnson

Day 10

Embrace Change

"The pages of your past cannot be re-written, but the pages of your tomorrows are blank."
—Zig Ziglar

Did you wake up this morning dreading the day? Or did you wake up expecting something new?

I don't know about you, but I don't want to run away from the new things God wants to do in my life. Look at the new thing as a challenge and an opportunity to grow. I remember working at a local restaurant as a waitress when I was a young woman of 19. The day came when they transitioned to a new computer system. This would allow for waitresses to take orders by memory and then input them into the new system and do away with paper. I panicked and thought, "What if I can't do this?" Because I feared the new thing and all of the emotions that went with it, I QUIT! I didn't even try or give myself the opportunity to see if I would fail or succeed.

I wonder how many of God's people are stuck in a place of stagnation because they have decided not to embrace change. If you intend to grow past the place you currently find yourself in, then you must be willing to embrace the opportunity in front of you. God is moving. He is shifting some things around for you and doing some new things on your behalf. Be willing to say "YES." Be willing to loosen your grip on the familiar and on your comfort zone. If you want to grow and be all that you were created for, then you must let go and trust God! Do not let fear grip you. Fear can mean two things: "Forget Everything And Run!" or "Face Everything And Rise!" The choice is yours. Change is up to you. How bad do you want it? It's okay if you fail; failure is not final unless you choose to stay down. If you're too afraid to fail, then you may never know the potential you carry.

Today, as you live in the present and look to the future, remember that God has an amazing plan for you. Act—and believe—accordingly.

Pause and Reflect:

1. Can you recall a time, like I can, when you were afraid to try something new? If yes, what was your reaction?

_____

_____

2. Do you feel stuck right now in a place of fear or stagnation?

   _____

   _____

3. Are you willing to give God your Yes, trust Him, and embrace the new thing He desires for you?

   _____

   _____

4. What steps would this require?

   _____

   _____

Go Deeper:

Isaiah 12:2 (NLT), 1 Chronicles 28:20 (NLT), Isaiah 43:18-19 (NLT), Jeremiah 29:11 (NLT)

Worship Encounter:

"Never Give Up" by Fearless Soul

"Fearless" by Jasmine Murray

"Say I Won't" by MercyMe

DAY 11

DIRT UNDER THE RUG

"Mistakes are always forgivable, if one has the courage to admit them."

—*Bruce Lee*

What are you sweeping under the rug?

Tough question, huh? A question that we don't want to answer because when we do, we have to face the dirt. It's easier to leave it hidden. You can't see it, and neither can anyone else. The only problem with that is, you know it's there, and so does God. It may be okay there for a while, but sooner or later, we have to deal with it.

So many times, we become victim to what we perceive as reality. But when we surrender our lives totally to God, then we give Him permission to pull that rug up so we can see the dirt.

Over 33 years ago, I went through a divorce from a very short-lived marriage right out of high school. For most of the years following, I blamed everything on my ex-husband, taking no blame for myself whatsoever. That was my reality. As the years passed, I surrendered my life more and more to God, growing and maturing in Him as He began to open my eyes to see truth. The true reality was that I needed to ask for forgiveness. It was such a humbling, but freeing moment for me to come to this realization. Once I faced the hard reality that I was just as much to blame, God gave me the unexpected opportunity to ask for forgiveness. To my surprise, God had done a work in my ex-husband's life as well, and he graciously offered the forgiveness I so needed. Suddenly there was TOTAL FREEDOM!

NO MORE DIRT, only a clean floor to dance with VICTORY on the enemy's head.

I think, if we can be honest with ourselves, we probably all have some kind of dirt under our rug. Maybe yours isn't a divorce. Maybe it's an argument with your best friend that needs to be healed, or it could be a misunderstanding with a family member. Whatever your situation, I feel God wanting to give you a clean floor of freedom and victory today.

Pause and Reflect:

1. Have you perhaps been sweeping something under the rug that you are reluctant to deal with?

_____

_____

2. Is there someone that you may need to apologize to and ask for forgiveness?

   _____

   _____

3. Ask the Lord to show you if you have become a victim to what you perceive as reality, and then ask Him to show you the truth.

   _____

   _____

GO DEEPER:

James 4:10 (AMP), Colossians 3:13 (AMP), Ephesians 1:18 (AMP), Proverbs 28:13 (TPT)

WORSHIP ENCOUNTER:

"I Surrender" by Hillsong Worship

"Blameless/How He Loves" by Dara Maclean

"Dancing on the Grave" by Naomi Cantwell & Christ for the Nations Worship

Day 12

The Crucible

"When God is on your side, no trial in life will be too much for you to overcome."
—**Samuel Zulu**

Trust God in the midst of the crucible.

Here are some of the essential meanings of "crucible" according to Merriam-Webster:

- A ceramic pot in which metals or other substances are heated to a very high temperature or melted.

- A difficult or severe test or challenge.

- A place or situation that forces people to change or make difficult decisions.

Any time spent with the Lord is exciting for me, whether it's 4 AM, 5 AM, 6 AM, or late at night before I go to bed. It's an exciting and interesting journey every single time. I never know where the journey will lead for that day or which turn He will decide to take. Each new journey is a learning experience because I discover something new about myself. Sometimes I like the new discovery, and other times it's quite unpleasant. Sometimes I find myself back in the crucible. It's very hot and uncomfortable, and sometimes the process is lengthy, but God is melting away all of the impurities so that the true me, the pure me, and the new me has been purified.

> "Let trials in your life guide you and not define you."
> —Kim Cormack

If you find yourself in the crucible today, allow the process to be completed no matter how hard or how hot it gets. Be encouraged that the Lord, the Refiner, never leaves your side during the refining process. You are way too precious and valuable for Him to allow you to be destroyed. When all of the impurities have been melted away, you come forth brand new! When this trial is over and the Refiner looks at you, He will only see His reflection. When you are in this place of being purified, you have to encourage yourself. So go ahead and grab hold of these I Am's and begin to declare them over yourself out loud:

I am fearless! I am confident! I am God's chosen vessel! I am an overcomer! I am holy!

I am enough! I am wanted! I am loved! I am beautiful! I am a worshiper! I am smart!

I am blessed! I am trustworthy! I am faithful! I am a finisher! I am an inspiration!

"Let trials in your life guide you and not define you."
—Kim Cormack

Be encouraged today and continue with your own declarations! Know that you are not alone in the crucible. You will come through this situation a new person, reflecting only His Image.

Pause and Reflect:

1. Have you ever been on a journey with the Lord and then He took an unexpected turn?

   _____

   _____

2. Sometimes the heat of a trial makes us feel like we are going to be destroyed. Can you describe a time when you felt this way?

   _____

   _____

3. Describe what the new you looked like after the refining process.

   _____

   _____

Go Deeper:

Proverbs 17:3 (TPT), James 1:1-4 (TPT), 1 Peter 1:6-7 (NLT), Deuteronomy 1:8 (AMP)

Worship Encounter:

"Refiner" by Maverick City Music

"Fires" by Jordan St. Cyr

"Overcomer" by Mandisa

"Another in the Fire" by Hillsong United

DAY 13

TRANSFORMATION!

"Perhaps the butterfly is proof that you can go through a great deal of darkness yet become something beautiful."
—**Anonymous**

I used to think that isolation was a bad thing, until I went into a season of isolation for myself. I tend to look at it a little differently now and see that it's not always a bad thing when the Lord is in it. Sometimes we isolate ourselves from others because we don't want them to know that we are dealing with past hurts and dwelling on events that have taken place in our lives. When we isolate like this, it can lead to oppression and depression. It can cause us to sink into a deep pit of despair and hopelessness.

Transformation!

Today, I want to encourage you to shift your perspective and focus on God, on His goodness, and on His purpose for your life: who He says you are, what He says you can do, and what He says you can become.

Sometimes God will allow us to go into a place of isolation just like that of a caterpillar in his cocoon, wrapped up in a dark place. That's often how we feel: alone in a dark place. What happens to the worm in the dark place is private between him and his Maker. There is a beautiful process called transformation taking place. When the process is complete, he breaks out of that place, transformed into a beautiful butterfly, ready to spread his wings and fly. Your Creator is doing the same for you.

If you find yourself in a place of isolation today, don't fight the process. He has you wrapped up in His presence, and He's doing an amazing and marvelous work on the inside of you. What is being prepared in the dark will soon be revealed in the light. When the time comes for you to break out, you must be willing to let go of the worm mentality and begin to see yourself flying with beauty. Let God complete the work that He has begun in you.

Pause and Reflect:

1. If you find yourself in a place of isolation today, God wants you to see the beauty, not the pain. Ask Him to change your perspective. Ask Him to help you let go of old mindsets that tell you nothing will ever change.

   _____

   _____

Write Out Your Own Prayer:

_____

_____

_____

_____

Go Deeper:

Philippians 1:6 (AMP), 2 Corinthians 3:18 (AMP), Romans 12:2 (TPT)

Worship Encounter:

"Changed" by Jordan Feliz

"Different" by Micah Tyler

"Beautiful, Beautiful" by Francesca Battistelli

DAY 14

THE R.A.W. TRUTH: REAL, AUTHENTIC, AND WORTHY

"Authenticity starts in the heart."
—Brian D'Angelo

This past week, I've gone through open heart surgery. Not the way most people would presume—I wasn't admitted into the hospital, nor was I put to sleep with anesthesia. Rather, I was at home, fully awake, and yes, I felt the pressure as my chest was cut open. I am very grateful that I had the best surgeon in the whole world. He knew that the surgery was necessary in order for me to continue to live. He knew that the surgery might go a little long and the recovery might linger a bit. Unlike me, He knew what He was facing, and He was prepared. He knew that this was going to be a painful process, and as He laid out His tools, He knew exactly which one to use at the proper time. As He massaged my heart, blood began to flow, and suddenly it began to beat again.

The R.A.W. Truth: Real, Authentic, and Worthy

This is the R.A.W. Truth!

There is a time when we have to get *real* and *authentic* with ourselves, and at the same time know we are still *worthy* of God's love.

> Definitions:
>
> Real (adj.): not imagined, not artificial, not an imitation but genuine.
>
> Authentic (adj.): not false or copied; genuine; real: representing one's true nature or beliefs; true to oneself. Authentic carries the connotation of authoritative confirmation that things or people are what they are claimed or appear to be.
>
> Worthy (adj.): having worth or value; someone or something that has desirable qualities and is entitled to respect or attention.

Sometimes being real is anything but pretty. In fact, it can be pretty messy and downright scary. You wonder who this person is and where she came from. Left alone to herself, she can be disruptive and destructive. This is one of the results of taking our eyes off of the one who created us and not reading the instruction manual He left behind. This is exactly where I found myself.

The instruction manual is like a map that guides you along every path that needs to be taken on your journey and gives you the necessary tools to use when there are detours and delays along the way. When you choose not to read the map, you enter into unchartered territory without the proper voice of guidance. Those places can be dark, treacherous, and life threatening. You cannot see in the dark, and shadows begin to appear. Your mind begins to race, and you begin to imagine things that aren't even there. Oh, but when you dig deep into your satchel and pull out that map, all of a sudden there is light that illuminates the darkness and drives out everything that was lurking and unclear. This instruction manual I'm referring to is the Bible.

Being authentic demands responsibility: a responsibility to ourselves and to those around us. Authenticity has cousins called character and integrity, which can be defined as who you really are when no one is around. When we get real and let God reveal truth about ourselves, we begin to question our authenticity.

The enemy is so good at getting us to question and doubt who we really are, but let's get one thing straight and settled: You are unique because your Heavenly Father broke the mold He crafted you from. You cannot be copied, nor should you try to copy or pattern your life by any other person than Christ Jesus. You are created in His image and likeness. Now it is time to rise and live like it! Be an authentic representative of the One you say you believe. So, the question is, who are you choosing to believe today?

For myself writing this, and for you who are reading this right now: no matter what you go through, no matter if you laid down the instruction manual and chose to take your own path, no matter if you chose to believe the lie over the truth, no matter if you compared yourself to another, know today that you are still WORTHY. It's not about anything that you did right or anything that you didn't do. It's all about what HE DID! You are worthy because He is worthy! You are righteous because He is righteous! What does that mean? You are in right standing with Him because He is seated right where He belongs, at the right hand of the Father forever making intercession (praying) for you.

Live from a R.A.W. place and know all will be well.

I am waking up from recovery. I am resting and allowing the Great Physician to heal all of my wounds. Today I declare: I am real! I am authentic! I am worthy!

Pause and Reflect:

1. Do you feel that there are areas where you need to be real and authentic with yourself?

   _____

   _____

2. Have you chosen to believe a lie over the truth?

   _____

   _____

3. Describe a time in your life when you chose not to follow God's instruction manual. What was the result?

   _____

   _____

Go Deeper:

Hebrews 4:12 (TPT), Psalm 143:8 (TPT), Psalm 37:23 (AMP)

Worship Encounter:

"I Look to You" by Selah

"Tell Your Heart to Beat Again" by Danny Gokey

"No Matter What" by Ryan Stevenson

DAY 15

FLIP THE SCRIPT!

"'For I know the plans and thoughts that I have for you,' says the Lord, 'plans for peace and well-being and not for disaster, to give you a future and a hope.'"
—Jeremiah 29:11 (AMP)

Have you ever felt on certain mornings as if you were handed two scripts to read—one negative and the other positive, one from the enemy himself and the other from the Holy Spirit? At that moment, you have the choice of which narrative you will follow that day. You get to decide which direction your day will take. Let's think about these two scripts for a moment and Flip the Script right here and right now.

> "Don't minimize the greatness of your God! "

The devil is a liar! He has no authority in your life!

Don't minimize the greatness of your God!

Don't allow the voice of Satan to be louder than the voice of God. Satan will suggest things to you all day long, but you do not have to get into agreement with him. Get into agreement with what God is saying and has already said about your life.

Remember, the enemy can't read your mind. He locates you by what's coming out of your mouth. This is why it's so important to renew your mind daily with the Word of God and let it sink deep down into your spirit. When you do this, the Word of God will come out of your mouth, and the Word will fight its own battle. Your whole life will be totally transformed by doing this.

Will it happen all at once? Absolutely not—that's why we must make it a daily practice. Will you always feel like doing it? Absolutely not, but do it anyway. It's the best investment that you can make for your life.

When Jesus died, you died with Him. When Jesus arose, you arose with Him. When Jesus sat down at the right hand of the Father, you sat down with Him. We have gained access to authority, but most of us either don't realize it or we just choose not to walk in the authority given to us. You have authority over the enemy!

For us to have authority, it comes through perfect union with Jesus, so we must abide in Him. To abide means to dwell: to align your thoughts, choices, and perspective under God's thoughts, choices, and perspective. It means connecting with Him and honoring Him in everything that we do.

Pause and Reflect:

1. We've all been guilty of involving ourselves in the wrong storyline. Can you describe a time you chose the wrong narrative?

   _____

   _____

2. Are you ready to Flip the Script on the enemy?

   _____

   _____

3. What steps will you actively take in this process?

   _____

   _____

Go Deeper:

Romans 12:2 (AMP), Luke 10:18-19 (AMP), 1 Peter 5:8-11 (AMP), John 15:4-5 (TPT)

Worship Encounter:

"First" by Lauren Daigle

"I Refuse" by Josh Wilson

"Speak Life" by TobyMac

DAY 16

Don't Back Down!

"You will never possess what you were unwilling to pursue."

—Mike Murdock

Make a declaration today that you will not back down! Back down from who? Back down from what?

First of all, don't back down from the enemy. I'm not referring to a person, I'm referring to Satan. He comes as a hungry lion to kill, steal, and destroy. BUT... God comes to give you life, and that more abundantly.

You see, the enemy comes in many shapes, forms, and fashions, even as an angel of light. One of his main weapons is distractions, which again comes through many means. These distractions are to get your eyes off of your purpose and onto the circumstances and situations surrounding your life. It's time to eliminate things (distractions) that don't add value to your life or your calling.

Secondly, don't back down from what God has called you to do. He has placed greatness on the inside of you, and He is well able to perform those things through you. Get refocused and recognize those things that are pulling you from your purpose! Lock eyes with the Promise Keeper! The key to possessing your promise is *Consistency* and remaining *Steady*! The promise is in the passionate pursuit! Today, declare out loud, *I Will Not Back Down!*

Pause and Reflect:

1. What is it that you feel God is calling you to do?

   _____

   _____

2. Can you identify some distractions that are causing you to back down from this calling?

   _____

   _____

3. How can you prioritize your life and minimize distractions to align with the purposes of God?

   _____

   _____

Go Deeper:

John 10:10 (AMP), Philippians 1:6 (AMP), Hebrews 12:1-2 (AMP)

Worship Encounter:

"Stand My Ground" by Zach Williams

"No Turning Back" by The Belonging Co. (feat. Hope Darst)

"This Is Freedom (Ain't No Rock)" by The Belonging Co. (feat. Natalie Grant)

DAY 17

HOLD THE ROPE

"When you're at the end of your rope, tie a knot and hold on."

—Theodore Roosevelt

The first sermon I ever heard my previous pastor preach was titled "Hold the Rope." He handed out little pieces of rope with knots on the end. After 30 years, I still have that rope. His message has helped me so many times, not only through my personal life, but as the Lord has used it to help me minister to others. In that sermon, he said, "No matter how hard life gets, tie a knot at the end of that rope and hold on for dear life." I want to encourage you today to put your hope and trust in the Lord. If you hold on and don't let go, you can be sure that things will change. Sometimes it's not the way we expect things to change—it could be just a change in our perspective. I do know that if we let God take care of it, He always works it out for our good. It's in the process that we learn who we are and who He is. Be refreshed today, knowing that He hasn't forgotten you. He knows where you are, and He is working on your behalf right this minute. So go ahead and tie a knot at the end of your rope and hold on—help is on the way!

> *"I'll never forget the trouble, the utter lostness, the taste of ashes, the poison I've swallowed. I remember it all—oh, how well I remember—the feeling of hitting the bottom. But there's one other thing I remember, and remembering, I keep a grip on hope:*
>
> *GOD's loyal love couldn't have run out, his merciful love couldn't have dried up. They're created new every morning. How great your faithfulness! I'm sticking with GOD (I say it over and over). He's all I've got left.*
>
> *GOD proves to be good to the man who passionately waits, to the woman who diligently seeks. It's a good thing to quietly hope, quietly hope for help from GOD. It's a good thing when you're young to stick it out through the hard times.*
>
> *When life is heavy and hard to take, go off by yourself. Enter the silence. Bow in prayer. Don't ask questions: Wait for hope to appear. Don't run from trouble. Take it full-face. The 'worst' is never the worst."*
>
> —Lamentations 3:19-30 (MSG)

Pause and Reflect:

1. Have you ever felt like you were at the end of your rope, or do you feel that way right now?

   _____

   _____

2. How would things change if you truly knew that God hasn't forgotten you and He is working things out for you?

   _____

   _____

3. Are you willing to allow God to change your perspective concerning your situation?

   _____

   _____

Go Deeper:

Genesis 16:13 (NLT), Deuteronomy 31:8 (NLT)

Worship Encounter:

"Hold On" by Riley Clemmons

"Hold On to Me" by Lauren Daigle

"Don't Lose Hope" by Cochren & Co.

DAY 18

RELINQUISH CONTROL

"I can rest in the fact that God is in control. Which means I can face things that are out of my control and not act out of control."
—**Lysa TerKeurst,** *Unglued*

If we could change life's situations, then why would we even need God? The truth is, we can't. We can't change situations or outcomes, and we definitely can't change a person's will—only God can do that.

We like to control our environments. We try to control the things that are happening to us and around us. Trying to make things happen or figure it all out only leaves us tired and stressed out. Today is a great day to relinquish that control. It may be true that your situation does not look favorable right now. It may look like things will never change; it may look utterly hopeless. You may have even said, "I guess this is how my life is going to be from now on." If you find that you have entered into a new season and your life looks totally different than what you planned, know that God is BIG ENOUGH to handle it and He will give you the grace to carry on. When you relinquish control, then He will release rest for your weary soul.

Let the Lord refresh you today! Allow Him to blow upon the embers of your heart so that it can be reignited with the passion that you carry.

Pause and Reflect:

1. Can you identify the season of life you are in?

   _____

   _____

2. Are you trying to control a situation or a person in your life?

   _____

   _____

3. Are you willing to relinquish that control to God?_____
   Can you agree that you will find rest and peace in that decision?

   _____

   _____

Go Deeper:

Matthew 11:28-30 (TPT), Philippians 4:6-7 (TPT), Psalm 42:11-12 (TPT)

Worship Encounter:

"Control" by Tenth Avenue North

"Control" by For King & Country

"Out of My Hands" by Jeremy Camp

DAY 19

PAUSE AND BE STILL

"I am humbled and quieted in your presence. Like a contented child who rests on its mother's lap, I'm your resting child and my soul is content in you."
—Psalm 131:2 (TPT)

Quietness /ˈkwaɪətnəs/
noun
Absence of noise or bustle
Synonyms: calm, hush, restfulness, peace, still, pause

I have to admit it's not easy for a woman like me to be still and quiet. "Busy" has always seemed to be my middle name! I also have to admit that this has gotten me into trouble as I have allowed unnecessary stress to enter my life. But lately, I've learned the art of slowing down, saying no to things and people, and simplifying my life. It's been uncomfortable at times, but I've learned to like it. In order for us—me, for sure—to go deeper, de-stress, focus, and gain a new perspective, we have to stop the fast-paced "merry-go-round" life. It's only then that we are able to see the little things that matter most in life.

I actually love the quietness. I've learned that life goes on even when my to-do list is incomplete. I've learned that what I get accomplished in a day does not determine my success or define who I am. My success is determined by my obedience to God alone. If I please Him, that's all that matters. I've learned that life goes on when I don't agree with other people's decisions, and even when they don't understand or agree with my decisions. I've learned that I can't fix everyone's problems. Oh, how I wish I could fix the world's problems, but after all, I'm not Superwoman. I've learned that I can't live up to everyone's expectations, nor can I hold on to disappointment because someone didn't meet my expectations. I've learned the beauty of letting go. I've learned the value of money and how quickly it can be stripped away when it's not stewarded well. I've learned that no matter how busy I am, how much time I spend trying to figure things out or try to fix things, maybe it's not meant for me to figure out or fix.

Let's face it, we live in a technology-driven world that is fast paced, busy, and very noisy. It's full of distractions, obligations, and frustrations.

If we allow our lives to continue on fast-forward, all of the important things and details of life get missed. Sometimes I wish I had a pause button that I could hit. The truth is, it's a decision that we have to make. We have to slow down, catch our breath, and relax in God's presence. It's important for us to be present in the moment. The Lord longs to visit with us, speak with us, and show us things. My husband often says, "Being busy for God can't replace our time spent with God." Let's not be so busy that we miss our visitation with the Lord.

In God's presence there is peace and joy, but so many times we allow the busyness, frustrations, and distractions of life to rob us of that peace.

Today, let God set the tempo of your life. As you relax and breathe Him in, let Him set the pace for your day. Quiet moments with God transcend all time, accomplishing far more than you could ever imagine.

Pause and Reflect:

1. Have you been so busy with life's demands that you have forgotten how to live in the moment?

   _____

   _____

2. Can you sense the Lord longing to spend time with you in the quietness? _____
   Take a moment now to let Him refresh you in His presence.

   _____

   _____

3. Take time to write down all of the things that are robbing you of your time and peace. Submit it to the Lord and ask Him for new strategies to eliminate those things from your life.

_____

_____

Go Deeper:

Psalm 46:10 (TPT), Psalm 131:2 (TPT), Isaiah 30:15-18 (NLT), 1 Kings 19:11-12 (AMP)

Worship Encounter:

"In the Secret" by Chris Tomlin

"Still" by Hillary Scott & The Scott Family

"Be Still" by Hillsong Worship

DAY 20

R.I.P.—Rest in Peace

"When things change inside you, things change around you."

—Unknown

On the morning of August 26, 2019, I was preparing myself to face the day that would include paying my final respects to my precious aunt as we laid her down for her final rest. I began to think about the words "Rest in Peace," a phrase often used when a loved one, or anyone for that matter, passes away. As I began to ponder upon this phrase, I realized that God wants us to R.I.P., Rest in Peace, every day. It's a peace that the world can't give. If the world didn't give it, then the world can't take it away either. That is true, but we often forfeit our peace. I'm talking about the peace of God. This is a peace that doesn't worry or stress about anything. It's a supernatural rest. God wants us to rest, not to overload our schedule to the point of exhaustion and feel overwhelmed with unmet expectations. Instead, He wants us to focus on His presence. When we pursue His presence, there is peace that guards our heart and our mind. Your circumstances may not have changed, but you will have a peace in the midst of it. Choose today to Rest in Peace—His peace.

> *"Do not be anxious or worried about anything, but in everything [every circumstance and situation] by prayer and petition with thanksgiving, continue to make your [specific] requests known to God. And the peace of God [that peace which reassures the heart, that peace] which transcends all understanding, [that peace which] stands guard over your hearts and your minds in Christ Jesus [is yours]. Finally, believers, whatever is true, whatever is honorable and worthy of respect, whatever is right and confirmed by God's word, whatever is pure and wholesome, whatever is lovely and brings peace, whatever is admirable and of good repute; if there is any excellence, if there is anything worthy of praise, think continually on these things [center your mind on them, and implant them in your heart]. The things which you have learned and received and heard and seen in me, practice these things [in daily life], and the God [who is the source] of peace and well-being will be with you."*
> —Philippians 4:6-9 (AMP)

Transcend

verb

Go beyond, rise above, surpass, excel, exceed, outshine, go beyond all limits. To triumph over the negative, to overcome.

Pause and Reflect:

1. Are you resting in the peace of God today?

   _____

   _____

2. What are some areas in your life where you have forfeited your peace?

   _____

   _____

3. What are the things that you are allowing your mind to think on?

   _____

   _____

   Today, replace any negative thought that is robbing you of peace and rest.

Go Deeper:

John 16:33 (NIV), Ephesians 6:18-19 (TPT), 2 Peter 1:2 (NLT)

Worship Encounter:

"Peace" by Danny Gokey

"God of Peace" by Nikki Moltz (feat. Josh Barnett)

"Give Me Your Peace" by Gateway Worship

"Peace" by Bethel Music

DAY 21

SEASONS

"There is a season (a time appointed) for everything and a time for every delight and event or purpose under heaven."

—**Ecclesiastes 3:1 (AMP)**

A few years back, while I was going through a Bible study called "I Do Hard Things" by Havilah Cunnington with some ladies from church, the Lord began to speak to me about seasons. I felt like He began to show me that just as we have our natural seasons of winter, spring, summer, and fall, this is how our lives are as well. I began to envision the hardness of the winter, the dead and dried-up places, those places that aren't producing any life. Then I began to see the seed that had been planted begin to burst forth from the ground and flowers begin to bud.

As I pondered on this, I began to think about the body of Christ. I, myself, may be going through a spring where everything is blooming, everything is beautiful, the sun is shining, and the birds are singing at my windowsill. But I may look over at my sister next to me, and she may be going through a harsh, cold winter. She may be going through a hard time in her life that looks like everything is dead around her, it's dried up, and there is no life in sight. She has lost her momentum, and there seems to be nothing to rejoice about.

As the body of Christ, we should encourage and lift one another up, especially in times like these. While I'm going through my spring or summer season, I can be the one who comes alongside my sister to encourage her to keep going, because she will see the sun shine again and this cold, hard season that she is facing will come to an end. The day will come when she is in her spring or summer season, while my season has changed to fall and it looks like my life is falling apart, just like the leaves falling from the trees. It's at that time that she can come alongside me to help me get through this transitional season.

> "Every season brings with it an opportunity for growth."

I think it's amazing how the Lord created our seasons, and if we can see it from this perspective, I believe He uses it as a model for the church to follow in caring for one another. I pray that you feel encouraged today knowing that whatever season you're in, He is there, and you don't have to go through it alone. The enemy would like for you to hibernate just as the bear does during the winter, but I would encourage you to worship through whatever season you find yourself in. Every season brings with it an opportunity for growth. Let's grow together.

"Try to be a rainbow in someone's cloud."
—Maya Angelou

Pause and Reflect:

1. In your own words, can you identify what season of life you are in?

   _____

   _____

2. Do you see an opportunity for growth during this season?

   _____

   _____

   If so, how?

   _____

   _____

3. Can you think of a friend who may need your help to get through a difficult season?_____ If so, what action can you take?

   _____

   _____

Go Deeper:

Hebrews 10:23-25 (TPT), Genesis 8:22 (NIV), Isaiah 58:11 (NLT)

Worship Encounter:

"Seasons Change" by United Pursuit (feat. Michael Ketterer)

"Desert Song" by Hillsong Worship

"Seasons" by Hillsong Worship

DAY 22

THE GREATEST COMMANDMENT

"The doctrines of Jesus are simple and tend all to the happiness of man, that there is only one God and God is perfect. That God and man are one. That to love God with all your heart, and your neighbor as yourself, is the sum of religion. These are the great points on which I endeavor to reform and live my life."
—Thomas Jefferson

Have you ever just paused long enough to really think about what is most important in your life? Is it your career, your car, your house, or your bank account? Or could it be your children, your grandchildren, your spouse, or maybe even a best friend? In all of these things I've listed, you'll notice I didn't mention God. Many times, great importance is put on everything else and God is an afterthought, when in fact He should be the most important. The Word reminds us of what should be most important.

The Greatest Commandment

> *"Teacher, which is the most important commandment in the law of Moses?' Jesus replied, "'You must love the Lord your God with all your heart, all your soul, and all your mind." This is the first and greatest commandment. A second is equally important: "Love your neighbor as yourself."'"*
>
> —Matthew 22:36-39 (NLT)

This is a commandment that is found eight times in scripture. God knew that we would struggle with this, so obviously He felt that He needed to repeat himself. I don't know about you, but this can be a major struggle for so many people, especially when that neighbor isn't being so kind. As I look back over that scripture, I see that He didn't ask us to love our neighbor, He *commanded* us to love our neighbor.

When we are loving our neighbor, we are actually loving God. We are living out what is most important.

When we make God the most important priority in our lives and obey His second commandment as the first, we are capable of obeying all of the commandments as listed in Exodus 20:2-17.

Pause and Reflect:

1. Take some time right now and think about what you have placed the most importance on in your life. Write down your top priorities in order.

_____

_____

2. Looking at this list, can you say without a doubt that God is most important?

_____

_____

3. Who do you consider your neighbor?_____
Do you find it hard to love them?_____ If so, continue with the prayer below.

_____

_____

Pray This:

Father, I ask you to forgive me where I have placed other things before you. Help me to put things in right perspective and in correct order. Help me to see others the way you do, so that I may love them well. Help me to realize that as I love them, I am honoring you and putting you first. From this day forth, I choose to put you first in all things. May you be glorified in all that I say and do. Amen!

Go Deeper:

1 John 3:18 (NLT), Matthew 6:33 (TPT)

Worship Encounter:

"Build My Life" by Pat Barrett

"First" by Lauren Daigle

"Neighbour" by VERSES

DAY 23

GOD IS CLOSE TO THE BROKEN-HEARTED

"If your heart is broken, you'll find God right there; if you're kicked in the gut, he'll help you catch your breath."
—**Psalm 34:18 (MSG)**

As I sat in my quiet place this morning, thoughts began to flood my being of a young girl who passed away at the age of 19 this week in the community I grew up in. Although I did not know her, I do know her parents. My heart began to break for them as tears welled up in my eyes and soon began to stream down my face, knowing that yesterday they said their final goodbyes. I can only imagine the pain they must be feeling as they wake up this morning, the day after. It has to be so overwhelming. I pray, Father, that you wrap them both in your loving arms, giving them comfort like only you can.

Death is never easy, whether young or old, whether you knew it was coming or it snuck up unexpectedly. The truth is, it comes for all of us. When I was younger, I didn't think of death that much. You tend to think you're invincible and you have your whole life to live. As I get older and death is all around me more and more, it's hard not to think about it. It's hard to know the words to speak to those who have lost someone. How could you possibly know the extreme heartache and sorrow they feel? Saying "I'm sorry" seems so hollow and inadequate. Most of the time, words aren't even needed; just being there for them is enough. For you and me, or anyone we know who is experiencing loss, the best comfort is found in God's Word. It tells me that God is close to the brokenhearted, those crushed in spirit, and those weighed down under the heavy load of sorrow. He hears us when we are crying out to Him, and He says that He will rescue us. It comforts me to know that the pain and sorrow I may be feeling today won't last forever. But while I'm in it, He sees me right where I am. He promises to never leave us nor forsake us. Each of us is so very precious to Him, and He stays close to us even in death. There is nothing, absolutely nothing, that catches Him by surprise.

> *"Not even a sparrow, worth only half a penny, can fall to the ground without your Father knowing it. And the very hairs on your head are all numbered. So don't be afraid; you are more valuable to him than a whole flock of sparrows."*
> —Matthew 10:29-31 (NLT)

GOD IS CLOSE TO THE BROKEN-HEARTED

PAUSE AND REFLECT:

1. Consider what helps you feel God's presence. If you don't feel it today, maybe you have in the past. How did His presence impact you then?

   _____

   _____

2. Think about a time in your life when you lost someone close to you. How did you get through that season?

   _____

   _____

3. Reflecting on the two previous questions, can you say that you knew the Lord was close to you?

   _____

   _____

   How can you use those experiences to help a friend who may be brokenhearted?

   _____

   _____

Go Deeper:

Psalm 34:17-18 (NLT), Psalm 116:15 (NLT), Deuteronomy 31:8 (NLT)

Worship Encounter:

"Why God" by Austin French

"The Garden" by Kari Jobe

"Scars in Heaven" by Casting Crowns

"Rescue" by Lauren Daigle

DAY 24

DON'T DISQUALIFY YOURSELF!

"Accept yourself, love yourself, and keep moving forward. If you want to fly, you have to give up what weighs you down."

—**Roy T. Bennett**

So many times, we do not see ourselves like others see us. We see ourselves through a flawed lens or a cracked mirror. We see ourselves by the things we have gone through or the mistakes we have made in life. Let me take a moment to tell you that you may have done things in your past that you are not proud of, but those things do not define who you are. Don't disqualify yourself based on past experiences.

Years ago, I served as a leader in our youth department at church. I cut out some hands on construction paper and taped them to the backs of every youth. I had each of them go around with a Sharpie and write one positive word that they saw in that person.

As the youth began looking at all of the positive things that were said about themselves, they were not only shocked but also encouraged. I then told each of them to put that hand somewhere they would be able to see it daily, and when they started thinking negatively about themselves or allowed the enemy to accuse them, to just say, "Talk to the hand."

> "Talk to the hand."

That may seem like a silly thing to do and say, but the truth is, so many of us, just like those youth, don't realize our value and how others truly see us.

I'm reminded of a friend who sent me a video message for my birthday. She began to tell me all of things she saw in me. It went like this:

"You have such a sweet spirit, you are transparent, you are a woman of integrity, you are a risk taker and I love that about you. You are kind, you are steady and firm, you are faithful (a faithful friend and faithful to your people), you are gentle, you are firmly established, you are strong in principle and character, and you are merciful."

It so blessed and encouraged me that my life had impacted her in such a way. It was a positive affirmation that canceled out every lie of the enemy that told me anything to the contrary.

You may not have a hand to put on your back for people to write on or a friend to tell you what they see in you, but what you do have is a Heavenly Father that affirms and approves of you every single day, so much so that He wrote a love letter about you and to you in His Word. His Word is not a flawed lens or a cracked mirror; instead, it's a perfect reflection of who He is and who you are. You are who God says you are.

Pause and Reflect:

1. How do you see yourself?

   _____

   _____

2. Can you accept positive affirmations from others, or is it hard to believe those things?

   _____

   _____

3. Would you dare to believe that you have great qualities and be bold enough to live them out each day?

   _____

   _____

4. Pray and ask the Lord to show you those for whom you can begin to speak positive affirmations into their lives.

   _____

   _____

Go Deeper:

James 1:23-25 (TPT), Philippians 1:6 (AMP), 1 Peter 2:9-10 (AMP)

Worship Encounter:

"Priceless" by For King & Country

"You Say" by Lauren Daigle

"Who You Say I Am" by Hillsong Worhip

"Define Me" by Jonny Diaz

Day 25

Entangled

"The cords of death entangled me, the anguish of the grave came over me; I was overcome by distress and sorrow. Then I called on the name of the Lord: 'Lord, save me!'"

—**Psalm 116:3-4 (NIV)**

At some point in our lives, we have all had to deal with the issue of unforgiveness, whether for ourselves or another person. There are many things we could probably say are easy to forgive. But what about that one thing that seems unforgivable? That one thing that seems to haunt you and won't let you forget it. I've had a personal journey with this very real issue. I've always considered myself a very merciful, compassionate, and forgiving person. Anyone who truly knows me would testify to that. When faced with a particular hurtful situation, I guess I could say that I hadn't lived long enough to experience all that life was going to throw at me.

There is a saying that comes to mind when we talk about this: "You never know what you might do when you're backed in a corner." The other thing that comes to mind is an illustration my husband uses with a glass of water. He says, "You can say this is water, but if bumped or knocked over, what's truly inside is going to come out. After all, it could be bitter, like vinegar." When you think of this illustration, if indeed it's vinegar, not only will it spill out and make a mess, it will stink, and above all, if you taste it, it would be sickening and make you cringe. Sometimes our lives look like this. On the outside, it looks like we are carrying the right thing, but on the inside, things are going terribly wrong.

I can look back on my life during this season of uncertainty as I was holding unforgiveness and see how it was like a glass of clear liquid that looked clean, pure, and refreshing. The truth is, inside, there was a lot of bitterness that I had allowed to get entangled around not only my heart but also my mind. The only way to describe it and give you a true visual is from the scene in the movie *Jumanji*, towards the end where these huge jungle vines took over the house. They grew very rapidly and wrapped around everything in a huge tangled mess with the intent to kill. Just like those vines, unforgiveness had me in a death grip. I knew I was in trouble when I had allowed myself to walk into this trap that the enemy had so strategically set for me. Escaping was not easy—it was a fight for my very life. My only hope was returning to what I knew to be true, and what had so freely been given for me in my transgressions: Jesus and His Word! If you find yourself entangled today, He is the only way of escape.

Pause and Reflect:

1. Can you describe a time in your life when you refused to forgive although you knew it was the right thing to do?

   _____

   _____

2. What did that decision lead you to, and how did it affect your life?

   _____

   _____

3. Have you been able to experience the redemptive work of the Lord in your life in this situation?

   _____

   _____

4. If not, ask the Lord to help you recount the cost at the cross that was paid for your redemption.

   _____

   _____

Go Deeper:

Psalm 91:3 (TPT), Psalm 124:7 (TPT), Ephesians 4:32 (NLT), 1 John 1:9 (NLT)

Worship Encounter:

"Forgiveness" by Matthew West

"A Heart That Forgives" by Kevin LeVar

"Where Forgiveness Is" by Sidewalk Prophets

Day 26

Basking in His Presence

"Nothing in or of this world measures up to the simple pleasures of experiencing the presence of God."
—A.W. Tozer

I remember years ago, when I really began a serious walk with the Lord, I would go on trips with my pastor's wife from time to time. I could never understand why in the early morning hours, she would sit alone at a table with her coffee, quiet, not saying a word. What could she possibly be doing? As I've grown in the Lord, I've come to the understanding that it was a privilege and an honor to be able to sit there quietly. What I didn't realize then was that she was communing with her Heavenly Father. She was basking in His presence and intently listening for Holy Spirit to speak to her. Now that I am older and more mature in the Lord, I look forward to those kinds of mornings as well. On cold winter mornings, I long to sit and warm by the fire, listening to it crackle as it dances through the fire logs, wrapped up in a soft, cozy blanket as if Holy Spirit Himself were holding me. On spring mornings, I love sitting outside on my back patio with a cup of coffee, admiring the beauty of the nature He created for me, listening to the birds as if they were singing a song just for me as they jump from one tree limb to another.

There are many things that I can live without, but the one thing I could never live without is His presence. God's presence is one of the most beautiful and most important things that we should all desire. His presence can bring peace to your troubled mind and comfort to your hurting heart. His presence can also bring joy to your life and clarity to all decisions you need to make. Having an intimate relationship with Him causes you to long for those times when you can just bask in His presence.

Pause and Reflect:

1. Can you remember the last time you just sat in the presence of the Lord? If not, what do you feel holds you back?

   _____

   _____

2. Do you desire God's presence above all else in your life?

   _____

   _____

3. If you find yourself in a place today where you are needing peace and direction, I encourage you to find a quiet place to pour it out to God. He's already there waiting to comfort you and speak to you.

_____

_____

Go Deeper:

Psalm 16:11 (AMP), Psalm 27:4 (AMP), Psalm 139:7-8 (NLT), Exodus 33:14-16 (NIV)

Worship Encounter:

"Oh the Glory" by Deeper Worship (feat. Matt Gilman)

"In the Presence of Jehovah" by The Martins

"Here in Your Presence" by New Life Worship

DAY 27

BEGIN WITH THANKFULNESS

"Gratitude is the ability to experience life as a gift. It liberates us from the prison of self-preoccupation."
—**John Ortberg**

> "When we cultivate a heart of gratitude and thanks, we begin to see life differently."

The Lord has been speaking to me a lot lately about having a thankful heart—a heart full of gratitude, one that is void of complaining. When we cultivate a heart of gratitude and thanks, we begin to see life differently. Oh, things may not have changed in our circumstances and everything may seem to be the same, but the way we view them has changed. We can so easily get caught up in the web of grumbling and complaining, seeing the worst of every situation and, sadly to say, even the worst in some people. We know where grumbling and complaining got the children of Israel. Yep, wandering around in the desert for 40 years when it was only supposed to be an 11-day journey. Can you imagine 40 years going around the same mountain? I have personally known some people with real struggles, seeking deliverance, seemingly going around the same mountain year after year, believing their victory is right around the corner. Not only have I seen it in other people, I've actually experienced it in my own life once or twice. I can honestly say that what was coming out of their mouth, and my own mouth, was more than half of the problem.

Grumbling and complaining keeps us focused on the problem, but when we are thankful and grateful, we are focused on the Problem Solver. When we adopt an attitude of gratitude and stop complaining, we are more aware of others around us. We develop a keener sense of hearing, which allows us to discern what they are speaking. Our attitude could very well be the magnet that draws people to the heart of God. It could also be the light that allows them to see their own attitude. People will begin to notice a change in you. When you cultivate this type of attitude, you become attractive to others, and you will be a very pleasant person to be around. The more you begin to express your thanks, the more you will find to be grateful for. As you develop this lifestyle, not only will you feel better as a person but it will have a positive effect in your relationships, your job, and your overall physical and spiritual health. Friend, I believe you and I both want to possess everything that the Lord has promised us. It begins today with thankfulness.

Pause and Reflect:

1. Take a moment and think about something that happened this week, this month, or even this year that you were grateful for.

   _____

   _____

2. Thinking back to yesterday, are you able to see the beauty in the day and recall something that made you smile?

   _____

   _____

3. Today, as you begin to develop an attitude of thankfulness, think about a negative that you are able to turn into a positive.

   _____

   _____

4. Write down three things you are thankful for today.

   _____

   _____

"When I started counting my blessings, my whole life turned around."

—Willie Nelson

Go Deeper:

Hebrews 12:28-29 (TPT), Exodus 16 (NIV), Philippians 2:14-16 (NLT), 1 Thessalonians 5:18 (AMP), Psalm 86:12 (TPT)

Worship Encounter:

"Thankful" by VERSES

"Grateful" by Elevation Worship

"Gratitude" by Brandon Lake

DAY 28

YIELD MY HEART

"When you yield yourself in complete and wholehearted obedience to God, He can do great things through you."
—**Jim George**

God wants a yielded heart that will make room for Him to come and do whatever He wants to. So many times, we think that we know what's best for our lives, but He holds the ultimate plan and He's already been in our future, so He definitely knows what's better for us. Sometimes we get tired in the waiting for those things we have been praying for, and we decide it would be better to go back to Egypt (meaning the old lifestyles He delivered us out of).

> "Yielding and surrendering yourself to God is the ultimate act of trust!"

None of our well-laid-out plans can even come close to the things that God has prepared for us. Yielding and surrendering yourself to God is the ultimate act of trust! Why do we make trusting God so hard? Everything we need is in His Word. His

Word has the final say in our lives. When I tell my 14-year-old son Ethan something, he trusts me and believes what I tell him. He'll have to remind me sometimes of things I've said, and he holds me to my word. How much more can we trust and believe our Heavenly Father who gave it all for us? We can remind Him of His word because He is faithful.

I encourage you today to lay it all down in total surrender and remain focused on the promise.

Pause & Reflect:

1. Has there ever been a time when you decided to go back to an old lifestyle? If so, how did it make you feel?

   _____

   _____

2. Do you find it hard to trust God with your future?

   _____

   _____

3. Why or why not?

   _____

   _____

4. God is tugging on you today to once again yield your heart to Him, letting Him take full control. Write out your own prayer of surrender to Him.

_____

_____

Go Deeper:

Jeremiah 29:11 (AMP), Isaiah 30:15-16, 18 (NLT), Proverbs 14:12 (TPT), Proverbs 16:9 (TPT)

Worship Encounter:

"Yield My Heart" by Kim Walker-Smith

"Make Room" by Community Music

"Better Than I" by Joy Williams

"Egypt" by Bethel Music

DAY 29

DISTRACTIONS! DISTRACTIONS!

"Until my ONE thing is done, everything else is a distraction."

—Gary Keller

This morning, I woke up feeling like a spiritual giant. I was focused on the day ahead of me, feeling pretty good about my schedule. I grabbed my first cup of coffee, Bible, devotion, and journal and sat down by the fire to begin reading. I knew this was going to be a special time in the Lord's presence. As I began reading, a thought came to my mind about a dear friend I haven't seen or heard from in a while. I knew she was on social media but had not seen any of her posts lately. Surely the Lord must be laying her on my heart—or was He?

As I picked up my phone to search her out, I saw a post from another friend requesting prayer for her son, so of course, I replied. Another friend was celebrating her daughter's accomplishments;

DISTRACTIONS! DISTRACTIONS!

again, I replied. Another friend posted a TikTok video of her daughter celebrating becoming a teenager; again, I replied. As I continued to scroll, I came across an ad to help women over 50 get the peach fuzz and dead skin off of their face. By all means, I needed that. Not only did I continue to watch the entire video, I stopped and made the purchase. Immediately after that, another video came on of a lady making a praying hands candleholder—surely I needed to learn how to make that.

By this time, the dogs outside were scratching at the door. They too have a schedule to keep, and it was their morning feeding time. "While I'm up, I might as well get that second cup of coffee," I thought. "Oh yeah, that friend, let's see if I can find her now." As I sat down a second time, I got around to finding her. Yes, there she was. It was good not only to see her face but to hear her voice as well. She had posted a video just a few days before, and actually, it was her video that I needed to hear.

This devotion really isn't about my friend; it's about all of the distractions that I allowed to enter my prayer time and get in my way while attempting to find her. When I looked at the clock, two hours had gone by since I had sat down to spend my time with the Lord. Two hours of distractions!

As I picked up my devotion for a second time, I reread the scripture I had previously read two hours before, but this time, it became a revelation to me:

> *"My heart has heard you say, 'Come and talk with me.'*
> *And my heart responds, 'Lord, I am coming.'"*
> —Psalm 27:8 (NLT)

My heart was grieved, and I can only imagine what the Lord was feeling. As much as I longed to sit down and talk with Him, there was so much that He wanted to tell me as well. Even in my wanderings and through all of the distractions, the Lord was gently waiting for me to turn my attention back to Him. It was comforting to know that His promises are true that He will never leave us or forsake us, even if we forsake Him. He wants us to seek Him with a whole heart, not a divided heart. Even in this, He was teaching me a valuable lesson.

Today, if you have found yourself distracted, give yourself some grace and know that God is bigger than any of your mistakes. Turn your focus and your attention back on Him—He is waiting for you.

Pause and Reflect:

1. Can you relate to a time when you went to the Lord in prayer but instead went to other things?

   _____

   _____

2. When we allow distractions to come between us and our quiet time with the Lord, do you feel that we are not fully trusting Him to meet our needs, or that He really isn't listening?

   _____

   _____

3. Speaking for myself, I find that bringing my phone into my prayer time is not always the best thing to do. What are some things that you could do differently in order to avoid distractions?

_____

_____

Go Deeper:

Deuteronomy 4:29-31 (NLT), Jeremiah 29:13 (AMP)

Worship Encounter:

"The More I Seek You" by Kari Jobe

"Here" by Tasha Cobbs Leonard

"Your Destiny" by Kevin LeVar

DAY 30

DON'T DESPISE WHERE YOU ARE

"Be faithful in small things because it is in them that your strength lies."
—**Mother Teresa**

Don't dismiss those fleeting thoughts. If you find yourself in a situation or ministry that seems menial or you feel as if you don't belong there, maybe God has you there in training for something greater. He could be doing a preparation work in you for that thing, or for that person or people. Before you try to kick your way out, ask the Lord for His plan and His purpose. Oh, we always have a plan and purpose, but is it His? During a recent Bible study with a special group of ladies, we journeyed through the life of Elijah. Elijah was sent to the most unlikely place, the Brook Cherith, a place in between where he was from and where he was going. It was an unlikely place, and God used the most unlikely way to sustain him.

You may feel like you are in an in-between place. You would never have chosen this place for yourself, but circumstances have forced you here. Don't try to run so quickly; don't despise this place. Instead, lean in to God. Although it may be uncomfortable at times, rejoice in the fact that God knows exactly where you are, He hasn't forgotten you, and He will sustain you during this season. This place, this process, is preparing you. Elijah was at the brook until God released him. He was now prepared for the greater thing that God was leading him to. Stay faithful right where you are until God releases you. I always say, "What's done in the flesh has to be maintained in the flesh." I want God's hand on everything I do. Where He guides, He will also provide—not only finances, but peace of mind and wisdom.

> "The real lessons learned in life are found in the process, not the final destination."

During my study of Elijah, I realized I had been at my own Brook Cherith. I had complained a lot of the time, but complaining wasn't changing my circumstances, and it was getting me nowhere except frustrated. I repented and once again surrendered my will to His. I've come to know that the real lessons learned in life are found in the process, not the final destination. Purpose is found in the process of your most unlikely place.

Pause and Reflect:

1. Just like Elijah and myself most recently, have you found yourself at your own Brook Cherith?

   _____

   _____

2. If you answered yes, then I know that you probably wouldn't have chosen this place. Do you feel that you are in a preparation process for something greater?

   _____

   _____

3. Are you willing to remain faithful where you are until God releases you?

   _____

   _____

Go Deeper:

1 Kings 17 (NLT), Psalm 119:50 (AMP), 1 Corinthians 15:58 (TPT)

Worship Encounter:

"If You Want Me To" by Ginny Owens

"Faithful" by Elevation Worship

"Where Would I Be" by The Belonging Co (feat. Hope Darst)

DAY 31

IT'S TIME TO POSSESS!

"I don't want to spend my whole life talking about the promised land without ever getting there. I want to live in it."

—**Joyce Meyer**

Have you ever been in a season where you felt like you were just wandering around? Or possibly just standing still, doing nothing?

Maybe you haven't wandered in the wilderness for 40 years like the children of Israel; maybe life hit you and you took a week's journey, possibly a few months or even several years. Maybe you have been in a season of standing still, and you're just watching life pass you by. Whatever the case and wherever you may find yourself today, the Spirit of God is saying this to you:

"No one will be able to stand their ground against you as long as you live. For I will be with you as I was with Moses. I will not fail you or abandon you."

—Joshua 1:5 (NLT)

It's Time to Possess!

It's time to start possessing! God has already gone ahead of you and prepared the way.

You've been faced with many challenges during your wandering season, but look at you, you are still standing! Your eyes are fixed and you refuse to quit. You have learned much! You've had to learn to be courageous and live by faith. And a consistent faith it will take to continue your journey.

In Joshua 18:2-3 (AMP), there remained seven tribes who had not yet divided their inheritance. So Joshua asked them, *"How long will you put off entering to take possession of the land which the Lord, the God of your fathers, has given you?"*

Whatever new challenge you face today, know that God is on your side! God does not lie, forget, change His words, or leave His promises unfulfilled.

Be STRONG and VERY COURAGEOUS—this is a command from the Lord your God. Go and take possession of what the Lord has already provided for you.

This is your time! This is your season to possess your promise!

Pause and Reflect:

1. Do you feel that you are or have been in a season of wandering or standing still?

2. Why do you feel that you procrastinate in doing the thing that God has asked you to do?

   _____

   _____

3. What are some lessons that you have learned during your wandering season?

   _____

   _____

4. How can you encourage others in their wandering season from your own experience?

   _____

   _____

Go Deeper:

Deuteronomy 1:5-8 (NLT), Numbers 33:53 (NLT), Psalm 33:4 (NLT), Jeremiah 30:1-3 (NLT)

Worship Encounter:

"Way Maker" by Sinach

"Possess the Land" by Embassy Worship

"Crossover" by Travis Greene

DAY 32

FROM PAIN TO PURPOSE

"You can be pitiful, or you can be powerful, but you can't be both."

—Joyce Meyer

Don't allow the pain of yesterday to paralyze your today and steal your purpose for tomorrow. Your greatest struggle to live a life of joy, peace, and strength is not with another person; the struggle lies within yourself. When you wake up in the morning, there is no one there telling you that you can't get up and do something. It's just you and the Holy Spirit. The Holy Spirit is our great "Paraclete," meaning one called alongside of us to help and comfort us. God is for you, not against you.

So, we have then to ask ourselves this question: "What's the problem?" What happens is that we allow our thoughts to get in agreement with the thoughts that the enemy is throwing at us. The darts, meaning thoughts, will be thrown at you all day long. But here's a word of advice: the enemy cannot read your mind. The only power he has over us is what we give him through what we are saying. So, when a dart comes, choose to pull it out before it has time to penetrate.

> "We cannot be pitiful and powerful at the same time."

We cannot be pitiful and powerful at the same time, so we must choose which we are going to be. Let's take a look at the definition of both:

Pitiful: Very small, inadequate, distressing, sad, pathetic, miserable. Causing feelings of dislike or disgust by not being enough or not being good enough.

Powerful: Having great strength. Strong, solid, sturdy. Powerful suggests the capability of exerting great force or overcoming strong resistance. A powerful machine like a bulldozer.

Wow! I know which one I want to be. How about you?

Instead of allowing the pain of yesterday or past failures to paralyze you to remain pitiful, choose to get up and become powerful with your God-given purpose.

Pause and Reflect:

1. Whether recently or in times past, have you allowed failure or pain to paralyze you? Explain.

_____

_____

2. Reading over the definitions of "pitiful" and "powerful" again, which do you identify with more today and why?

   _____

   _____

3. You don't have to live pitifully. As you choose a powerful life today, write out your own declaration as you pursue your purpose.

   _____

   _____

Go Deeper:

1 John 4:4 (NLT), Ephesians 3:20 (AMP), John 5:1-9 (AMP)

Worship Encounter:

"Stronger" by Mandisa

"Greater" by MercyMe

"Up Again" by Dan Bremnes

DAY 33

TAKE OFF THE LIMITS

"God puts dreams in your heart that are bigger than you so that you will rely on Him and His power."
—**Tony Evans**

I remember when I was a little girl and growing up into my teen years, I had so many dreams, as many young girls do. As I began to get older and walk with the Lord, I realized that the dreams I had for my life weren't His dreams for my life. He began to give me glimpses into my future, and very honestly, it was scary. These were some pretty big things, and I knew that He would have to be the one to cause them to come to pass, because I could never do it on my own. I began to put limits on myself and question my ability to even move towards these things. After all, who was I, and what would people think?

One morning, the Holy Spirit gave me a vision of a huge sunflower field. The only thing that was between me and this huge field of never-ending sunflowers was a fence. The fence was old and wooden, low enough to cross over, and had slats wide enough apart for me to crawl through. The only thing stopping me from crossing over was me. God was saying, "There are no limits on my part—here it is for your taking. You have my permission and approval."

The limitations that I had were put there by my own doing, in my own mind. What if I did cross over? If I got scared or uncomfortable, I could very well jump right back over the fence to where I was, only to continue to look on and just dream of what could be. But what if I crossed over? Where would I go? Anywhere I wanted to go. What would I do? Anything I wanted to do. God already said He gave me His permission and approval. Nothing was holding me back.

If we never cross the fence, then we will never experience what life can be—all the things we could experience. And what about all of the people we would meet? We would forfeit the impact that we could have made on another person's life.

I chose to take the limits off and cross the fence. Today I challenge you to take the limits off as well and cross over whatever fence is standing between you and your dream.

God will prove Himself faithful to you when it is part of His plan for your life. He has financed every dream I have ever dreamed!

- Becoming a real estate agent
- Recording a CD
- Starting a business
- Adopting a child

These are just a few examples of God's provision. These dreams go much deeper than finances; they also hold much eternal spiritual value as well.

He has already promised provision for dreams yet to come to pass. If He did this for me, then He can do this for you. God shows no favoritism.

If you will dare to dream it, God will let you see it. After you see it, then go live it! Take off the limits!

> *"The moment God put the dream in your heart, He lined up everything you need to bring it to pass."*
> —Joel Osteen

Pause and Reflect:

1. Who or what are you allowing to limit you?

   _____

   _____

2. Are you willing to move in the direction of your dream?

   _____

   _____

3. Do you trust God to bring provision for your dream?

   _____

   _____

Go Deeper:

Philippians 4:13 (AMP), Psalm 105:19 (NLT), Proverbs 13:19 (NLT),

Philippians 1:6 (AMP), Acts 10:34(TPT)

Worship Encounter:

"I Will Trust" by Red Rocks Worship

"Dream" by Shirley Murdock

"No Limits" by Israel Houghton & New Breed

DAY 34

NOT FORGOTTEN!

"God calls each and every star by name. It's not likely He has forgotten yours."

—**Louie Giglio**

Have you ever felt forgotten, abandoned, or rejected? Somewhere along our journey, we have probably all felt this way at times. Sometimes we blame others for the way we are, the reason we act the way we do, or the reason we feel stuck in life. While we are feeling stuck and blaming others, those very people are moving on in life. The truth is, we all have to take responsibility for our own lives and choose to keep our hearts right before the Lord.

I don't think there's a better example of what I'm talking about than the life of Joseph. We find his story in Genesis 37-50. If anyone had a reason to feel forgotten, abandoned, or rejected, it would have been him. He could have easily become bitter about his situation, stayed stuck in life, and missed out on his destiny.

Joseph was favored above his brothers by his father. He had been born to his father, Jacob, in his old age. At the age of 17, Joseph was given a beautiful coat by his father, and his brothers hated him all the more. They couldn't even say one kind thing about him. His brothers wanted to kill him, but instead, they stripped him of his coat and threw him in a deep pit. They ended up selling him to a group of Ishmaelite traders, which in turn sold him to Potiphar, an officer of Pharaoh. After being wrongly accused by Potiphar's wife, he was thrown in prison.

While in prison, Joseph interpreted dreams for the baker and the cupbearer. The cupbearer promised not to forget Joseph after he was released. It wasn't until two years later, when Pharaoh needed a dream interpreted, that the cupbearer remembered him. When Pharaoh sent for him, Joseph must have known that his life was fixing to change. What he did next was key, and very important for us to remember. He got up, shaved, and then changed his clothes before going before Pharaoh. From that moment on, Joseph experienced much restoration in his life. In everything he went through, the Lord had been with him.

If you're feeling like life hasn't been fair to you, stop and think about Joseph. Just like Joseph, you are not forgotten. You must first make a decision to get up, then wash off anything that you have allowed other people to put on you, and next put on some new clothes as you approach your King. Don't allow what man has done or said to you keep you from reaching the destiny God has already prepared for you. You have potential and purpose—now rise up and go get what's yours!

PAUSE AND REFLECT:

1. Have you ever felt rejected by someone and stuck in life because of their actions?

   _____

   _____

2. Was there ever a time when you felt like God had forgotten or abandoned you in the middle of your pain?

   _____

   _____

3. Did you realize the purpose behind the pain?

   _____

   _____

GO DEEPER:

Genesis 50:20 (NLT), Romans 12:12 (AMP), Genesis 37-50 (NLT), Isaiah 44:21 (NLT)

WORSHIP ENCOUNTER:

"Not Forgotten" by Israel Houghton

"Better Than I" by Joy Williams

"Not Forgotten" by Ryan Stevenson (Feat. TobyMac)

Day 35

Find Your Anchor

"If God be our God, He will give us peace in trouble. When there's a storm without, He will make peace within. The world can create trouble in peace, but God can create peace in trouble."

—Thomas Watson

Sometimes the storms of life raging all around us seem to be tearing our boat apart. The winds are way too strong for our sails to keep us moving in the right direction, and we feel that our ship is going to sink at any moment.

There are all kinds of storms that we face through our journey: health, marriage, physical, financial, family, and emotional. At times, it seems like way more than we can bear. But through my own personal storms, I have found an anchor for my soul, and it's called hope.

Anchors have always been a symbol of the sea, and they represent hope and steadfastness. Anchors are typically connected to a boat/ship by a long chain for the purpose of holding the vessel in place. It keeps the ship from drifting and helps to add stability to it during a storm. These are the very things that we need in our lives. We need that anchor to hold us steady. June Hunt explains in *Hope: The Anchor of Your Soul*: "For centuries, anchors have been a symbol of hope. This emblem was especially significant to the early persecuted church. Many etchings of anchors were discovered in the catacombs of Rome, where Christians held meetings in hiding. Threatened with death because of their faith, these committed Christians used the anchor as a disguised cross and as a marker to guide the way to their secret meetings."

This is what the Word says in Hebrews 6:19 (AMP):

> *"This hope [this confident assurance] we have as an anchor of the soul [it cannot slip and it cannot break down under whatever pressure bears upon it]—a safe and steadfast hope that enters within the veil [of the heavenly temple, that most Holy Place in which the very presence of God dwells]."*

STEADFAST: dutifully firm and unwavering.

Synonyms: loyal, faithful, committed, devoted, dedicated, dependable, reliable, steady, true, constant, solid, firm, determined, relentless, unchanging, unwavering, unhesitating, unfaltering, uncompromising, unflinching. Steadfast in one's faith, standing firmly in place, not wavering. Someone can be steadfast in a belief, an effort, a plan, or even a refusal. Whatever it is, it means that the person will calmly hold firm to the chosen position and follow through with determination.

God is calling you to be steadfast today!

Pause and Reflect:

1. What personal storm do you find yourself in today?

   _____

   _____

2. Are you feeling tossed to and fro by the winds and waves of this storm, or do you feel God's peace in the midst of it?

   _____

   _____

3. Would you describe yourself as a person who is anchored and steadfast?

   _____

   _____

   Explain why or why not.

   _____

   _____

Go Deeper:

Psalm 107:28-29 (TPT), Mark 4:39 (NLT), Romans 15:13 (AMP)

Worship Encounter:

"Peacespeaker/Wonderful Peace" by Grace Brumley

"For a Moment" by Elevation Worship

"Peace Be Still" by Hope Darst

DAY 36

THE POWER OF CHOICE

"One decision is oftentimes the thing that catapults you into your purpose.... Don't waver in that decision!"
—**Unknown**

God will never interrupt the free will of man. We have the power of choice. But remember, the choices and decisions that you make affect not only the outcome of your life but also the lives of all those connected to you.

> *"Today I have given you the choice between life and death, between blessings and curses. Now I call on heaven and earth to witness the choice you make. Oh, that you would choose life, so that you and your descendants might live! You can make this choice by loving the Lord your God, obeying him, and committing yourself firmly to him. This is the key to your life. And if you love and obey the Lord, you will live long in the land the Lord swore to give your ancestors Abraham, Isaac, and Jacob."*
> —Deuteronomy 30:19-20 (NLT)

Yes! We have the power of choice. We can't often change or determine what happens to us on the outside, but we can change and determine what happens on the inside of us.

There were a couple different times in my life when I faced seasons of great difficulty and challenge in my relationships. I couldn't see anything but the situation I was facing. I didn't see how it could possibly ever change or get better. All I saw was devastation in my world. I couldn't feel anything but the emotional pain of what I was experiencing. There was torment in my mind day and night. During these seasons, I felt it would be best if I didn't even exist. In those moments of desperation, I had a choice to make. I knew I really didn't want to die; I just wanted the pain to end. I would often tell other people to never make a permanent decision in the midst of a temporary situation, and I was now the one having to live out my own words. What I didn't realize was that God was closer to me than He had ever been. Although He did not cause the things happening in my life, He was using them for a greater purpose. I just couldn't see it. All I had the strength to do was call out to Him for help, and He did just that. He came to my rescue. As He extended His hand to me while I was in that dark pit, I made the decision to get up.

> "You are one decision away from something new!"

When you make a decision to get up, the Lord will pick you up! Life is all about choices and making decisions. Most of the time, your circumstances will not change, but you don't have to allow those circumstances to change who you are. You are one decision away from something new!

If God allows situations in your life that you don't understand, just trust Him in spite of it. He has a purpose, a plan, and a reason for it. Don't allow adversity or someone else's bad decision to stop you from living. Stop waiting on other people to change in order for you to be happy. Your power to choose has authority over all things.

This is a brand new day! A gift from God! You only live once, so make a decision to get up today and live it to the fullest!

Pause and Reflect:

1. What is one area of your life that you need God to restore right now?

   _____

   _____

2. Explain an event or circumstance in your past that has dramatically shaped your current life in a positive way.

   _____

   _____

3. Who are the people in your life who look up to you?

   _____

   _____

   How do you think the choices you make might impact their lives?

   _____

   _____

Go Deeper

Habakkuk 3:18-19 (AMP), Romans 8:28 (AMP), 1 Corinthians 10:13 (TPT) Proverbs 3:5 (TPT)

Worship Encounter:

"I Thank God" by Maverick City Music & UPPERROOM

"You Restore Everything" by Rick Pino (feat. Abbie Gamboa)

"God Turn It Around" by Jon Reddick

DAY 37

GUARD AND HARDEN NOT YOUR HEART

"Guarding your heart means protecting deepest parts of who you are—both your emotional and spiritual worlds—from anyone who could cause them harm."
— **Debra Fileta**

"Guard your heart above all else, for it determines the course of your life. Avoid all perverse talk; stay away from corrupt speech. Look straight ahead, and fix your eyes on what lies before you. Mark out a straight path for your feet; stay on the safe path. Don't get sidetracked; keep your feet from following evil."
—Proverbs 4:23-27 (NLT)

This should be our lifestyle. In the hour and days we live in, we must be laser focused on God's plan for our lives and walk in that way. The enemy wants so much to come in and distract us from those purposes and plans. We need to make sure that our desires and affections stay in the right direction. We should learn how to put up boundaries on our desires so that we do not allow every little thing to come in, and in the same way, we should not go after everything we see. We must keep our eyes focused on the things of God so that we do not get detoured into things that bring destruction.

We should also guard our hearts and not allow them to be hardened by the cares of life. There is a place of rest that God wants to bring His people to, but we must hear His voice and not harden our hearts. The easiest thing for a person to do is get hard and bitter through times of strife and testing!

> *"O come, let us worship and bow down, Let us kneel before the Lord our Maker [in reverent praise and prayer]. For He is our God And we are the people of His pasture and the sheep of His hand. Today, if you will hear His voice, Do not harden your hearts and become spiritually dull as at Meribah [the place of strife], And as at Massah [the place of testing] in the wilderness."*
> —Psalm 95:6-8 (AMP)

The hardest thing to do is stay the course. But YOU, my friend, reading this RIGHT NOW, were made to do hard things. Stay tender to the things of the Lord, and do not allow your heart to get entangled with the affairs of this life. I encourage you to not to look to the left or to the right, but rather stay the course and watch as the garden of your heart flourishes with life.

TODAY is the best day to find peace with God.

Pause and Reflect:

1. Are there any roots in your life that may be stopping the garden of your heart from thriving?

   _____

   _____

2. Do you feel that you've allowed your heart to get hardened by life's trials?

   _____

   _____

3. Set aside some time to spend time with God and His Word to help you identify the roots that need to be tended to so that the garden of your life can thrive.

   _____

   _____

Go Deeper:

Exodus 17:1-7 (NLT), Numbers 20:1-13 (NLT), Philippians 4:6-7 (TPT), Psalm 119:11 (NLT)

Worship Encounter:

"Don't Let Your Heart Be Hardened" by Petra

"A Heart Like Yours" by CeCe Winans

"My Heart Is Yours" by Passion (feat. Kristian Stanfill)

DAY 38

THERE IS MORE

"Never doubt God's mighty power to work in you and accomplish all this. He will achieve infinitely more than your greatest request, your most unbelievable dream, and exceed your wildest imagination! He will outdo them all, for his miraculous power constantly energizes you."
—**Ephesians 3:20 (TPT)**

Have you ever asked yourself the question, "Is this all there is to life?" Surely, Lord, there must be more than this. I have definitely asked this question a time or two. I've also asked the Lord to show me the "more." If we are truly sincere when we ask the Lord those questions, He will sincerely show you. Let me take a moment to share an experience with you concerning the "more."

Several years ago, I had a beautiful gray cat named Macy Gray—and Macy was spoiled, to say the least. On one particular morning, I gave her only half of a can of cat food and put the other half on the counter. When I turned around moments later, she was on top of the counter with her nose in the can, trying desperately to eat the rest of the food. I said to her, "You knew there was more, didn't you? You weren't satisfied with just a little bit." I immediately heard the Holy Spirit speak to me and say, "That's how I want my people to be. I want them hungry for more. I don't want them satisfied with just a little bit because there is much more that I have for them. But they have to be hungry enough and desperate enough to go after it."

That simple example gave me a great revelation of the love that our Heavenly Father has for us. He doesn't want us satisfied with barely enough when He has so much more for us. He doesn't want us to become complacent when there is more for us to experience. This is where we can begin to see change in our lives, not only to be filled up with His goodness but to live in the overflow. You, my friend, have been created for more. You haven't been created to sit back and let life idly pass you by. The Creator of the universe breathed life into you. He breathed a plan, a purpose, and a destiny inside of you! So yes, my friend, there is more! Arise today and go after it.

Once you taste of His goodness, you'll never be satisfied with less.

Pause and Reflect:

1. Have you ever asked the question, "Is there more to this life?"

_____

_____

2. Take a moment to do a little examination of your life. Can you find areas where you have become complacent and satisfied?

   _____

   _____

3. Do you feel that there is something standing between you and the Lord that is stopping you from becoming more hungry and desperate for Him? _____ If yes, take a moment to repent and surrender it to Him so that you can experience all that He has for you.

   _____

   _____

Go Deeper:

Matthew 6:33 (TPT), Jeremiah 29:11-13 (AMP), Matthew 5:6 (AMP), Psalm 103:1-5 (AMP)

Worship Encounter:

"Come Taste and See" by Red Rocks Worship

"More" by Red Rocks Worship

"(There's Gotta Be) More to Life" by Stacie Orrico

DAY 39

PRESENT IN THE MOMENT

"Yesterday is history. Tomorrow is a mystery. Today is a gift. That is why it is called the present."
—**Alice Morse Earle**

Time is a very precious thing, and it's the only thing we can't get back once it's gone. I don't want to miss anything that the Lord has for me. Lately, He has been teaching me how to be present in the moment, and how to truly love and care for people for who they are and not for what they can do for me or how I can benefit from them. Sometimes we can fall into the busyness of our day-to-day tasks and somehow fail to realize that we're missing the best part of life. Especially for those in ministry like myself, we tend to overlook the daily opportunities of connection: the very thing that the Lord craves for us to have with others, relationship.

So, what does the best part of life look like? It looks like being present in the moment. It looks like cultivating a life of peace. It looks like cultivating friendships for eternity. It looks like inviting someone to your table. It looks like taking time to sit with them and being able to look into their eyes to not only see the pain, but hear the pain in their voice as they speak, to truly hear their heart. Many of them feel so very alone and don't want to burden other people with their problems. Often they have thoughts of "Who wants to listen or even take the time anyway?" So they decide to carry the burden alone and bury it deeper and deeper on the inside. Many of them don't want you to try to fix them; they just need you to listen to them.

There's a lot going on in people's lives that we'll never know about unless we take the time to be present in the moment. Oftentimes when we slow down and learn this rhythm of life, our souls get nourishment that we didn't even realize they needed. Learning how to be present in the moment and cultivate relationships is necessary for our vitality and a flourishing life.

Cultivate means "to prepare for the raising of crops," "to protect and encourage the growth of," "to cause to grow by special attention or by studying, advancing, developing, practicing, or publicizing." Part of the second definition speaks volumes: "to improve by labor, care, or study."

Synonyms: nurture, encourage, foster, care for

We don't accidentally cultivate; we purposefully cultivate. Cultivating takes work. It's a verb—an action word. We must actively and purposefully cultivate the things in our lives that we want to grow. My prayer today is that you and I focus on cultivating what matters.

Pause and Reflect:

1. Do you feel like your life is out of balance when it comes to your relationships?

   _____

   _____

2. What would being present in the moment look like to you?

   _____

   _____

3. How could your decision to slow down and be more present in the moment affect others around you?

   _____

   _____

Go Deeper:

Ezekiel 36:34-38 (AMP), James 4:13-15 (TPT), Matthew 6:34 (TPT)

Worship Encounter:

"Keep Me in the Moment" by Jeremy Camp

"Gifts from God" by Chris Tomlin

"Burdens" by Jamie Kimmett

Day 40

Victory in Every Season

> *"We thank God for giving us the victory as conquerors through our Lord Jesus, the Anointed One. So now, beloved ones, stand firm, stable, and enduring. Live your lives with an unshakable confidence. We know that we prosper and excel in every season by serving the Lord, because we are assured that our union with the Lord makes our labor productive with fruit that endures."*
> —1 Corinthians 15:57-58 (TPT)

As our journey together is coming to a close, my prayer is that you can easily say, "I am not defined by my struggle." Whether your season is summer or winter, one of joy or sorrow, you can have victory.

The Lord promises that He remains constant and unchanging. If I am in Him and He is in me, then I too am able to be firmly planted and steadfast. I can honestly say that I haven't always had steady emotions, but I can confidently say that I am not defined by the struggles of this life. I've always known where my help comes from and that I don't have to strive or fight for victory. Instead, I can live my life from a place of victory. I know the Victor who has made me victorious, and that same Victor makes you victorious too. There's a different position you can take when you know who you are and whose you are. Knowing who you are in Christ is your key to victory. When you know who you are, then you can't be defined by anything else. Your circumstances may shake you, but they don't have to shape you. Oftentimes we call ourselves "unshakable," but I would be lying if I said I've never been shaken. The truth is, is that I have been blindsided and caught off guard by certain circumstances of life, but I have never allowed myself to be removed from my position in Christ. Remember that after every storm, the sun does shine again.

> "When you know who you are, then you can't be defined by anything else."

Another thing I'd like for you to remember is that the beauty God brings forth in your life often comes from your most broken places. God doesn't want you to live from a broken place but rather a place of wholeness. Grab hold of the eyes of faith, see yourself as Jesus sees you, and see yourself in a different place. Just because you may have gone through difficult seasons in your life, that doesn't mean it's who you are. You are a child of God, a daughter or a son of the Most High. You are who He says you are, and you can do what He says you can do. There is no better time than now to start living the life God created you to live. Now is the time, this is the place, and you are the person.

"The one I love calls to me: Arise, my dearest. Hurry, my darling. Come away with me! I have come as you have asked to draw you to my heart and lead you out. For now is the time, my beautiful one. The season has changed, the bondage of your barren winter has ended, and the season of hiding is over and gone. The rains have soaked the earth and left it bright with blossoming flowers. The season for singing and pruning the vines has arrived. I hear the cooing of doves in our land, filling the air with songs to awaken you and guide you forth. Can you not discern this new day of destiny breaking forth around you? The early signs of my purposes and plans are bursting forth. The budding vines of new life are now blooming everywhere. The fragrance of their flowers whispers, 'There is change in the air.' Arise, my love, my beautiful companion, and run with me to the higher place. For now is the time to arise and come away with me."

—Song of Songs 2:10-13 (TPT)

Pause and Reflect:

1. On our last day together, I want you to go back to Day 12 and declare out loud the "I Am's." Now add "I am who you say I am" and "I am victorious in every season of my life."

_____

_____

2. As your beautiful Savior is calling you to come away with Him, journal out your final thoughts.

_____

_____

Go Deeper:

Psalm 121:1-8 (NLT), John 15:5-8 (NLT), Psalm 1:3 (TPT)

Worship Encounter:

"My Beloved" by Kari Jobe

"I Can't Get Away" by Melissa Helser

"Desert Song" by Hillsong Worship

www.ingramcontent.com/pod-product-compliance
Lightning Source LLC
Chambersburg PA
CBHW071119090426
42736CB00012B/1949